John Morris

Catholic England in Modern Times

John Morris

Catholic England in Modern Times

ISBN/EAN: 9783741187445

Manufactured in Europe, USA, Canada, Australia, Japa

Cover: Foto ©Lupo / pixelio.de

Manufactured and distributed by brebook publishing software (www.brebook.com)

John Morris

Catholic England in Modern Times

CATHOLIC ENGLAND

IN MODERN TIMES.

BY THE

REV. JOHN MORRIS, S.J., F.S.A.

LONDON:
BURNS AND OATES, LIMITED.

1892.

ROEHAMPTON:
PRINTED BY JAMES STANLEY.

CONTENTS.

			PAGE
CHAPTER	I.	The Revolution	i
,,	II.	The Eighteenth Century	17
,,	III.	Catholic Emancipation	34
,,	IV.	Our Component Parts	54
,,	V.	Our Hopes for the Future	73

Google

CATHOLIC ENGLAND IN MODERN TIMES.

CHAPTER I.

THE REVOLUTION.

THERE are few subjects at this moment agitated amongst us which equal in interest or importance the discussion of the condition and prospects of the Church in England. The differences of opinion on the subject are extremely great. With some it is all *couleur de rose*, with others our prospects are as black as they can be. Temperament has doubtless something to do with the conclusions arrived at on either side, and it may be well worth while to try to ascertain, from a quiet investigation of facts, where the truth lies. It concerns it greatly to know whether we have our lot cast in a winning or a losing cause, and our duties may be affected by the results. Facts alone are worth considering, and unhappily facts are not easily come by. We will do all that it is in our power to do, in order to come to a just conclusion, when we set ourselves to look into our own times. But first it will be worth our while to see from what we have emerged,[1] and then it will be well for us to examine our present condition, and to see how far it justifies us in being hopeful or alarmed. We will take our retrospect back a couple of centuries, and pass rapidly through our comparatively recent history, before we look at our present state.

The last two centuries may well be regarded as forming a distinct period in the history of the Catholic Church in England. The year 1688 is the date of the revolution which, through the national hatred of the Catholic religion, caused what was euphemistically called the "Abdication" of James II., and the transfer of the crown of England to the Protestant branches of the Royal Family. From the time of Henry VIII. to the accession of William and Mary, English Catholics had looked

---

[1] We are indebted for most of the facts given in this chapter, to the three books published by Mr. Orlebar Payne, *Records of the English Catholics of 1715*, *English Catholic Non-Jurors of 1715*, and *Old English Catholic Missions*; as well as to *The English Catholic Hierarchy*, by Mr. W. Maziere Brady. A general acknowledgment is better than a series of references.

for the recovery of the country to the Catholic faith by the succession to the crown of a Catholic, or the conversion of the reigning Sovereign. At last this contingency had occurred, and a Catholic sat on the throne of England. But the absolutism of the Tudors had gone, except indeed in the frantic theories of king-craft, summed up as in a principle, in the "divine right of kings." Nearly a century and a half of Protestant domination had obliterated from the mind of the nation all memory of the ancient Church that had Christianized the land. In the place of her fair image there was substituted in men's ideas an odious parody of the truth concerning her; and calumny, reiterated through generations of public and private teaching, made Englishmen hate what their fathers had loved and clung to. Any power for good that a Catholic King might otherwise have had, was thus entirely precluded, and, to precipitate a catastrophe, unwisdom may be said to have sat on the throne with the later Stuarts. All hope of the speedy conversion of England had vanished when these two centuries began.

The position of Catholics was then bad enough, but unfortunately circumstances led them to make it worse. As the authors of the Pilgrimage of Grace under Henry VIII., and of the Northern Rising under Elizabeth, gave their enemies an occasion to hang them wholesale in their towns and villages, and as the conspirators in the Gunpowder Plot played into Cecil's hands, and gave him a pretext for molesting innocent Catholics, so the unhappy campaign of the Jacobites in 1715 put the remnant of the English Catholics at the mercy of their adversaries, and the wonder is how any of them survived. There was something very beautiful in their loyalty. They had suffered in the Civil Wars for Charles I.; his son, Charles II., owed to Catholics more than to Protestants the preservation of his life and his restoration to the throne; false accusations, such as Titus Oates' "Plot," had robbed them of their lives, their liberties, and their reputations; Parliament, under the Stuarts, had clamoured for the blood of their priests; yet English Catholics had not swerved from their loyalty, and their enthusiasm led them to risk all that remained to them in behalf of the exiled family.

Their zeal cost them dear. The risings in behalf of James III. and his son Charles Edward, caused no doubt a temporary alarm to the Elector of Hanover, as the Jacobites called George I. and George II., but when the fright was over, the reigning powers must have rejoiced at what had happened, for it enabled them to bring a terrible pressure to bear on English Catholics. The authorities learnt wisdom in one respect from what had gone before. They did not shed on the scaffold the blood of priests, and of those who harboured them. There had been a century and a half of martyrdoms, from 1535, when Fisher and More and the Carthusians led the way, to 1680, when Thomas Thwing, priest, suffered at York, William Viscount Stafford in London, and 1681, when Oliver Plunket, Archbishop of Armagh, who died at Tyburn, gloriously closed the long line of our English Martyrs.

The Government was well advised, from its own point of view, in putting no more Catholics to death on the scaffold, with the exception indeed of such a man as the Earl of Derwentwater. Publicly inflicted martyrdom was an occasion when crowds of Protestants heard and felt the most impressive of sermons, when Catholics had their courage renewed, and went away proud of their religion, and when all nations were moved to sympathy with the victims of persecution. Imprisonment and fines were more effectual weapons, involving none of these drawbacks. They had been used freely from the beginning of Elizabeth's reign with fearful effect, and they were used not less freely on the weakened and broken remnant of English Catholics under the Prince of Orange and the first two sovereigns of the House of Hanover. Fresh legislation strengthened for their cruel work hands that were powerful enough already. Toleration was supposed to have been imported with the Prince of Orange, but it was toleration for all but Catholics. In the first Parliament of William and Mary an Act was passed to exempt their Majesties' Protestant subjects dissenting from the Church of England, and especially the Quakers, from the penalties of all laws made against them, and in it there was a clause that "Papists, Popish recusants, and such as deny the doctrine of the Trinity," were to receive no benefit by the Act.

A previous Act of the same Parliament, while it substituted a new oath of allegiance, renewed the oath introduced by James I., that the deposing power of the Pope is "impious and heretical," and that "no foreign Prince, Person, Prelate, State, or Potentate hath, or ought to have, any jurisdiction, power, superiority, pre-eminence, or authority, ecclesiastical or spiritual, within this realm." It also declared that any should be deemed a Popish recusant convict who should refuse to take the oath enacted in the 30th year of Charles II., the terms of which are that "there is not any transubstantiation of the elements of bread and wine into the Body and Blood of Christ at or after the consecration thereof by any person whatsoever, and that the invocation or adoration of the Virgin Mary, or any other saint, and the Sacrament of the Mass, as they are now used in the Church of Rome, are superstitious and idolatrous."

Another Act of the same session was "for amoving Papists and reputed Papists from the cities of London and Westminster and ten miles distance from the same."

Yet another Act of the same session of Parliament was "for the better securing the Government by disarming Papists and reputed Papists." This Act extended not only to arms, but to horses, forbidding any Papist to keep a horse above £5 in' value. The Papist who did not discover his arms to a Justice of the Peace, or who should conceal, or aid in concealing horses, was to be committed for three months without bail, and to forfeit three times the value of the arms or horses. Any two Justices could authorize persons, with the assistance of a constable, to search for arms or horses, and to seize them for the King's use.

There was still one more Act of Parliament in this session against Papists, vesting in the two Universities the presentations of benefices belonging to them.

All these Acts were passed in the first year of William and Mary. A more malicious Act than any of these was passed in the 11th and 12th years of the same reign. It enacted that whoever, after the 25th of March, 1700, shall apprehend a Popish bishop, priest, or Jesuit, and convict him of saying Mass, or exercising his function within this realm, is to receive of the Sheriff of the county for every such conviction £100, to be paid within four months, under penalty of £200 to be paid by the Sheriff in default. Every Popish Bishop, priest, or Jesuit, who shall say Mass or exercise his function, and every Papist keeping school, educating or boarding youth for that purpose, to suffer perpetual imprisonment. Persons educated in, or professing the Popish religion, but not their heirs or posterity, disabled to inherit or take any lands, tenements, or hereditaments within this kingdom; and during such persons' lives, until they take the oaths, the next of kin being a Protestant to enjoy his lands, without being accountable for the profits. Every Papist, after the 10th of April, 1700, disabled to purchase lands in this kingdom, or any profits from land. Whoever shall convict a person of sending his child beyond sea to be educated in Popery, to receive the whole penalty of £100 inflicted by the Act of James I. Popish parents of Protestant children refusing them a fitting maintenance, the Lord Chancellor to order as he shall think proper.

This Act might well be called "for the further preventing the growth of Popery." It was a weapon that, if vigorously used, would have served for its extermination. For the pursuivants who had been the priest-catchers in Elizabeth's time, and who after all were servants of the Crown, the common informer was now substituted. The penalty of £100 to be paid to any person who should obtain the conviction of a Catholic Bishop, priest, or Jesuit, was a strong inducement to any busybody to obtain information that could be made so lucrative. An apostate could employ his knowledge of Catholic chapels and priests to some purpose. One end was brought about by this Act which may have been directly intended by the Government. It practically substituted perpetual imprisonment for the penalties of high treason, which by the 27th of Elizabeth were the doom of "Jesuits, Seminary priests, and other ecclesiastical persons, born in these realms and ordained by the pretended authority of the See of Rome, who should come into or remain in the Queen's dominions." The informer could only benefit by laying his indictment under the Act of 11 and 12 William and Mary, and this he was sure to do.

Thus the Act under which the majority of the English Martyrs suffered was practically superseded, but it must be remembered that it was not repealed. It remained on the statute-book, part of the law of the land, and it hung over the head of every priest in the country. If the two Acts, one of which inflicted death and the other perpetual imprisonment on a priest for no other offence than being in England, did not root out the clergy altogether and thus cause the Catholic religion to die a natural death, it must have been due to the kindly feeling of Protestant neighbours, who though they thought Catholics elsewhere deserved every severity, yet looked on the handful of quiet people with whom they were acquainted, the Catholic squire who was a good landlord, and the tutor who lived in the squire's house and taught his children, but who was well enough known to be a priest, as exceptionally good Catholics, not to be molested.

Molested of course from time to time they were, and the right to search for arms and for horses, the uncertainty of what would come next, how old laws against them would be carried out and what new ones would be made, must have harassed them so that it is not to be wondered at that their numbers dwindled away. Men nominally conformed, and took the oaths by which their religion was abjured, in heart remaining Catholics and hoping before death to be reconciled to the Church. In Elizabeth's time they did it in the hope that, when her reign should end, a Catholic Sovereign might come to their rescue, and relieve them from the laws that crushed them. After the Revolution any man who did so, must have done it in despair, seeing no prospect of any change, at least after the failure of the Stuart rising in 1715. It was little to be wondered at that English Catholics should have thrown in their lot with the Stuarts. It was their one hope of relief; but when the first and most promising enterprise failed, they had but little hope of success for the second, and few Catholics comparatively speaking were involved in the dismal failure of 1745.

Not the least hurtful part of the cruel Act of William and Mary was the premium offered to children to become Protestants. In such a case they could apply to the Lord Chancellor for a maintenance out of their father's estate, and on his death the Protestant child became the heir, in preference to elder brothers who continued to be Catholics, and in contravention of the terms of the father's will. Indeed any kinsman could claim the inheritance if he were a Protestant and all the children Catholics. To what extent these powers were used we have not the means of ascertaining. Here however is an example, taken at hazard. Glover in his *History of Derby* says of a freehold estate called Whetstone in the parish of Tideswell that, "When John Alleyne died, a Mr. Freeman laid claim to the estate as Protestant heir and succeeded in wresting it from the infant." In other words a Protestant relative obtained it in preference to the Catholic heir, to whom it would have passed if he had been a Protestant.

The rising of 1715 brought down on the Catholics an Act of Parliament that placed their property still more in the power of their enemies. The 1st of George I. cap. 50 is entitled, "An Act for appointing Commissioners to inquire of the estates of certain traitors, and of Popish recusants; and of estates given to superstitious uses, in order to raise money out of them severally for the use of the public." The "certain traitors" were those who had been attainted for levying war, whatever their religion; and their estates were declared to be vested in the actual and real possession of His Majesty, without any inquisition found. The Commissioners appointed for this purpose were further to inquire the names of all persons who stood convicted as Popish recusants in England and Wales, and this in a summary way, without the forms of law. They were to report all the estates held by Catholics or by any persons in trust for them, thus including the cases where lands were held for Catholics by friendly Protestant neighbours. The Commissioners were to report the amount of the two-thirds liable to seizure by the Act of James I. when the King should prefer to take two-thirds of the lands of those who absented themselves from church instead of the forfeiture of £20 a month. And all property employed for any Popish or superstitious use was to be deemed to be forfeited to His Majesty "for the use of the public."

The list of the estates of the English Catholic nonjurors of 1715 has been printed in an interesting volume by Mr. Orlebar Payne. For our present purpose it will be sufficient to refer to a subsequent Act of the 9th year of George I., which tells us that a Report, signed by seven Commissioners under the Act passed, "to oblige Papists to register their names and real estates," was presented to the House of Commons in 1720, and in it the yearly rents of estates registered "amounted in the whole to £384,950 6s. 6¾d. over and above large sums arising from time to time for fines payable by leasehold and copyhold tenants." This Act, in lieu of all other pains and forfeitures, ordered that £100,000 should be levied on the Papists for the year 1723, over and above the double taxes to be paid by them.

The manner in which this sum is apportioned on the various counties is interesting as showing us where at that time the wealthiest Catholics were found. Naturally enough the county of York leads the way, having £12,974 allotted to it for payment as its share of the £100,000 to be paid by the Papists. Next comes Lancashire, assessed at £7,109. Stafford is third and Northumberland fourth, each taxed above £5,000: Lincolnshire, Sussex and Middlesex over £4,000 each; and Durham, Warwickshire, Northamptonshire, Staffordshire, and Norfolk over £3,000, in the order in which their names are here given.

We may now allow ourselves to leave the wearisome details of these persecuting Acts of Parliament, the enactments, be it remembered, of the period under our examination, for we have attempted no summary of the previous penal laws that were in full force at the Revolution. We may turn to inquire whether anything is known of the number and condition of English Catholics at that time. And first of all, as to their number. Mr. Madden, in his *History of the Penal Laws*, quotes from Sir John Dalrymple a curious official report, which was said to have been found after his death in the iron chest of King William III. It relates to freeholders only, and it gives the members of the Church of England under the title Conformists, and Dissenters of all sorts as Non-Conformists.

"Number of freeholders in England.

	Conformists.	Non-Conformists.	Papists.
Province of Canterbury	2,123,362	93,151	11,878
Province of York	353,892	15,525	1,978
	2,477,254	108,676	13,856
Conformists		2,477,254	
Non-Conformists		108,676	
Papists		13,856	
		2,599,786	

"According to which account the proportion of
Conformists to Non-Conformists is .. ... 22¼ to 1.
Conformists to Papists .. .. 178$\frac{19}{18}$ to 1.
Conformists and Non-Conformists together to Papists 186⅔ to 1."

Of the total number of Catholics at the time of the Revolution no data exist that would enable us to speak with certainty. In 1631, Panzani, who was sent to England by the Pope to report on the state of religion in England, said that there were 150,000 Catholics of all ranks, and he reckoned the secular clergy as about 500, the Jesuits over 160, the Benedictines 100, the Franciscans 20, Dominicans 7, Carmelites 5, and Minims 2, or in all 794 priests.

In 1669, a petition to the Pope numbered the Catholics as having risen to nearly 200,000, and the priests as 800. On the other hand, Agretti, who was sent by the Pope on a special mission to England in 1669, reported that there were 230 secular priests in divers parts, 120 Jesuits, 80 Benedictines, 55 Franciscans, a few Discalced Carmelites, and a few Dominicans. Agretti was but a short time in England and his figures are probably erroneous, but the discrepancy between them and those of Panzani throws doubt on all.

King William's estimate of freeholders is even less worthy of confidence. In his time such an estimate could be only guesswork, and this is a guess very wide of the mark. Mr. Madden calls it "an authentic document," and so it may be for all we know, in the sense that it really came from King William's strong box, but it is utterly untrustworthy. It gives a total of two millions six hundred thousand freeholders in England, at a time when the whole population of the country can hardly have exceeded five millions and a half. And as for the Papist freeholders being 13,856, 3,000 would be nearer the truth. When the estates were registered after 1715, the whole number of entries was 3,800, and amongst these the same name recurs in various counties, and the joint holders of an estate are all counted separately. Mr. Orlebar Payne has identified, among the freeholders here registering their estates, "the names of three bishops and some forty priests, although of course the troubles of the times in which they lived compelled them to conceal their office, so that there is nothing whatever in the records to indicate what they were."

The Catholics in England remained without the benefit of Episcopal government, ostensibly for thirty years and practically for fifty-six. Dr. Richard Smith was made Bishop of Chalcedon and Vicar Apostolic of England and Scotland in 1625, but the times were dangerous and he withdrew to France in 1629. A proclamation was issued in December, 1628, forbidding any one to harbour the Bishop, and another in March, 1629, in still more stringent terms decreed his banishment, and offered a reward of £100 for his capture. A curious story is told by Panzani, showing that the Bishop was for a time sheltered by the Marquis de Châteauneuf, the French Ambassador, and that Charles I. knew it. One day in Lent the King requested his wife, on account of her state of health, to eat meat, and as the Queen scrupled to do so without a dispensation, the King begged the Ambassador, who was then at Court, to send a servant home at once to get leave from the Bishop, adding that he knew very well that he would find the Bishop there.

The Bishop of Chalcedon died in Paris on the 18th of March, 1655. It was not till August, 1685, that Dr. John Leyburne, the President of Douay College, was appointed Vicar Apostolic of all England, with the title of Bishop of Adrumetum. He arrived in London in October, after his consecration in Rome, and King James II. lodged him in Whitehall, giving him a pension of £1,000 a year. The Bishop was accompanied by Ferdinand, Archbishop of Amasis, the Nuncio, and both of them were charged by the Holy See to oppose the King's policy, and moderate his endeavours to force Catholicism on a reluctant nation. Bishop Leyburne boldly told the King that the Fellows and Students of Magdalen College had been grievously wronged by the appointment of Dr. Giffard as President, but his advice had no weight with the King till it was too late.

In 1687, the Bishop visited the northern counties, and in four months gave Confirmation to 20,859 persons. It must not be forgotten, with regard to the largeness of the number, that no Bishop had visited these counties in the lifetime of the oldest person amongst them. The places so visited where Catholics were most numerous were Wigan, where 1,332 were confirmed, Preston 1,153, Euxton 1,138, Fernyhalgh 1,099, Naseby (his brother Urban Leyburne's place) 1,052, Croxteth 1,030, and Durham 1,024. Newcastle had only 360 confirmed, and Wolverhampton 37.

In January, 1688, Pope Innocent XI., at the request of James II., divided England into four districts, the King assigning to each of the new Bishops £1,000 a year and £500 on their first taking possession. Dr. John Leyburne became the first Vicar Apostolic of the London District, Dr. Buonaventure Giffard of the Midland District, Dr. James Smith, President of Douay, of the Northern, and Dr. Philip Michael Ellis, O.S.B., of the Western Districts. The three new Bishops were consecrated in London by the Papal Nuncio on the 22nd of April, the 6th and the 13th of May, the first of these ceremonies taking place in the Banqueting Hall at Whitehall, the second at St. James's, and the third at Somerset House. It was not in the power of James II. to carry out his good intentions as to their maintenance, for in November of that year he had to fly from England. He left behind him, however, a very beneficial legacy to the Catholics, who henceforward had four Bishops to take care of them.

When the King left the country, Bishops Leyburne and Giffard attempted to do the same, but they were arrested at Faversham and sent, one to the Tower, and the other to Newgate. There Bishop Leyburne was detained for two years and Bishop Giffard for one, while Bishop Ellis was imprisoned for a time in Newgate. The fourth Vicar Apostolic, Bishop Smith, had to leave York, but he was received and protected by Mr. Francis Tunstall, of Wycliff, till his death. His crozier was seized by the Earl of Danby, and it is now to be seen in York Minster.

Bishop Ellis went abroad when released from prison, and he never returned to England. In 1708, he was made by Clement XI. Bishop of Segni in the Volscian Hills, and there he died in 1726 after a useful Episcopate. A curious trace of his English title is found in the name by which he is called in inscriptions and records at Segni—Philip Michael Mylord Ellis.

It is to the credit of William III. that he should not have insisted on the banishment of the two Bishops who were his prisoners. Dr. Leyburne was allowed to live quietly in London, and on his death in 1702, Dr. Giffard was transferred from the Midland District to succeed him in that of London, in addition to the Western District, of which he had temporary charge.

In 1706, Bishop Giffard wrote to the Cardinal Prefect of Propaganda: "I have been for sixteen months tossed about in continual disturbances and perils, so as scarcely to find anywhere a place to rest in with safety." The Venetian Ambassador, Francesco Cornaro, gave the Bishop shelter for a year and more, for which service he received the thanks of the Holy See.

Again he wrote, in October, 1714: "Since the 4th of May I have had no quiet. I have been forced to change lodgings fourteen times, and but once have I lain in my own lodging. Besides the severe proclamation which came out on the 4th of May, three private persons have been, and still are, the occasion of my troubles. The first some fallen Catholic, who in hope of the great reward of £100 informed, and procured warrants for me, Mr. Joseph Leveson, and some others. The second is Mottram, who being expelled the University of Cambridge for his immoralities, got into Spain, there was entertained by the good Fathers at Seville, and in a very short time made a convert and priest; but no sooner in England than he became as loose and immoral as ever, and now to gain money for his wicked courses, is turned priest-catcher, and has got warrants for me and others. The third is one Barker, turned out of Douay for his ill-behaviour, received at Rome, made priest and sent hither; but always of so scandalous a life that no persuasions or endeavours could reclaim him. Nay, with much expense we sent him to our good community in France, where he was presently so infamous, especially for being frequently drunk, that they turned him out, and now being returned, he follows Mottram's tread. A few days ago he took up Mr. Brears, and has been in search of me and others; so that I am forced to lie hid as well as I can. I may truly say what was said by St. Athanasius, *Nullibi mihi tutus ad latendum locus*, whence I am obliged often to change my habitation. I have endeavoured to procure a little lodging in the house of some public minister, where I could be secure from the attempts of these wretches, but I could not effect it. My poor brother [Andrew Giffard, a priest who had refused the Western Vicariate in 1705], though much indisposed, was forced by the threats of an immediate search by Mottram, to retire into the country, which so increased his fever that in seven days he died. An inexpressible loss to me, to the whole clergy, and to many more.

"My service to Mgr. Bianchini and Marcolini. They saw my little habitation, poor and mean, and yet I should think myself happy if I could be permitted to lodge there. However, *gloriamur in tribulationibus*. I may say with the Apostle, *in carceribus abundantius*. In one I lay on the floor a considerable time; in Newgate almost two years; afterwards in Hertford gaol; and now daily expect a fourth prison to end my life in. I have always envied the glory of martyrs: happy if God in His mercy will let me have that of a confessor. Mottram took up Mr. Saltmarsh, but by a good Providence he got from him. The continual fears and alarms we are under is something worse than Newgate. It is also some mortification for an old man, now 72, to be so often hurried from place to place. God grant me eternal rest. I am yours, B. G."

The good old Bishop faced his troubles for another twenty years, dying at Hammersmith in his 92nd year, March 12, 1734. The two brothers, Buonaventure and Andrew Giffard, were buried in the same grave in that favourite burying-ground of Catholics, St. Pancras Churchyard.

The reward of £100 for the apprehension of a Catholic priest, with the higher value of money in those days, was enough to arouse the covetousness of the common informer, as it was intended to do. So also did the rewards given by the Commissioners of Forfeited Estates for a "discovery." The class of persons who availed themselves of their knowledge to obtain these rewards were the same in both cases. The informers were all but exclusively apostates from the Catholic religion, and in far the larger number of cases apostate priests. Trustees for Catholic pious uses were offered a fourth part of the estate, if they would betray them to the Commissioners, but to their honour none of them did so.

The informer who gave the Commissioners fuller information than any other was Richard Hitchmough, whom the Commissioners recommended to the Lord Chancellor "as a proper person to be preferred to some benefice in his lordship's gift. He formerly was a priest of the Church of Rome, but has left the communion of that Church about five or six years, during which time he has lived in extreme poverty and very much persecuted by the Papists, upon some occasions even to the hazard of his life. He is a man of good character," they write, "and has been hearty and zealous in his service to the public by giving us information in relation to estates settled to Popish and superstitious uses." Again they wrote, "He has a wife and several young children, and is extremely poor, and is still rendered more unfortunate by the continual vexation of the adverse party, too powerful in those parts," that is to say, at Liverpool, where the unhappy man then lived. He was accordingly appointed to the living of Whenby, in Yorkshire, a place we are told where half the parish was Catholic.

As a specimen of the extremely numerous informations given in by this man, we content ourselves with one. We will take Holywell, the famous chapel of St. Winefride in which place was given by the Queen to the Jesuits in 1688. The date, with the monogram IHS, may still be seen in the old stonework above the well. The mission had then been in the hands of the Society for a century, and from 1700 to 1802 there was a secular mission in the town as well. Each of the mission houses was an inn, and Hitchmough, in an information dated June 27, 1718, says "that the house in Holywell town, commonly called the Star, which is let by the Jesuits at £60 *per annum*, belongs to that Society, Mr. Griffiths being the present resident Jesuit there; and another house there called the Cross Keys, belongs to the secular clergy, Peter Bodwell, *alias* Girin, resident priest there." That very day the Commissioners, then sitting at Preston, wrote to the Major of the Regiment of Dragoons, commanded by Sir Charles Hotham, desiring him to detach such a number of soldiers under his command as he should think proper, seeing that "information has been laid before them that there are two Popish chapels at Holywell in which are a great quantity of plate and other valuables given to superstitious uses," and in consequence they had "directed their precepts to Richard Hitchmough, clerk, and others, to seize and secure the same." The informer gave in an inventory of the Church plate at the two missions that he had seen there nine years before. It may be worth giving at full length, to show what the generosity of Catholics could do for the altar, even in such times.

"At the Star: six large silver candlesticks, with a large silver crucifix on the altar. For solemn feasts, six large candlesticks with a crucifix, said to be of gold, with other plate answerable. On the middle of the altar, a large silver tabernacle, in which were kept a golden remonstrance, in which the Sacrament was exposed on great days: a large ciborium, out of which the priest communicated the people, one large gold chalice and paten, one large silver chalice and paten double-gilded and well-carved, with two others of a smaller size: a large silver basin, six silver cruets and four plates, which belonged to the side table by the altar: two silver thuribles, with which they incensed the Sacrament when exposed. In the middle of the chapel hung a large silver lamp before the tabernacle: in the vestry were lodged the shrines and large reliquaries, which contained, as they affirmed, part of the bodies of several saints, with which the altar was adorned on great days, besides rich copes, vestments, antependiums, and all church linen suitable, and also a library of books.

"At the Cross Keys, for common use, six tall candlesticks and crucifix of Corinthian brass, said to be as valuable as silver. Six large silver candlesticks and crucifix. In the tabernacle, which was ebony, were kept a large silver chalice well gilt, which was said to weigh three pounds, two silver chalices of a smaller size, a large remonstrance for exposing the Sacrament, and a ciborium in which the Sacrament was kept, besides cruets and other plate belonging to the altar. Two silver lamps hung constantly before the Sacrament, and there were two thuribles to incense it with. In the great chest and press in the vestry were reposited the Mass-books, vestments, and all other utensils for church use."

It is a comfort to know that the expedition was not very successful. Father Edmund Plowden wrote to Father Eberson on the 1st of August: "The Commissioners now sitting at Preston sent a party of dragoons with Hitchmore the fallen priest at their head to Holywell, where they plundered the two Popish chapels. The Star had pretty good luck, and got most of the effects out of the way in time. An old gentleman, Mr. Wilmot, was taken at the Cross Keys, but soon bailed."

Thomas Parry it appears was "innholder" at the Cross Keys, Robert Floyd at the Star. The device of an inn at which the priests lodged was an appropriate one for Holywell, as many pilgrims came there and it was convenient for them to be housed where they could have easy access to the priest.

Another specimen of the Commissioners' handiwork may be more briefly given. They report to the Right Hon. Robert Walpole "that upon inquiry they found that Thomas Eccleston of Eccleston, county Lancashire, was seized in fee of an estate at Eccleston to the yearly value of £352, and that being so seized, he about the 10th of October, 1700, became a Jesuit, and was by such profession, and the constitution of the Order of Jesuits, rendered incapable of holding any messuages, &c., to his own use, but to the use and benefit of the Religious House College, or Society of Jesuits, to which he belonged. By reason whereof we have found that the said messuages, &c., have been given by operation of law to Popish or superstitious uses. And we hereby certify that Richard Hitchmough, late of Preston, county Lancashire, but now of Whenby, county York, clerk, was the discoverer thereof."

When Father Eccleston petitioned that he might be heard by counsel, pleading "that his aged mother was reduced to want, being without any fault turned out of her habitation, and reduced to the utmost extremity," their answer was: "Let Mr. E. attend." This, being known to be a Jesuit, he did not dare to do.

Two other Jesuits, however, Robert and Charles Collingwood, grandsons of Henry, fifth Viscount Montague, trusting with good reason not to be known as Jesuits, appeared before the Commissioners claiming annuities, and saying that "there will be due to them each four years' arrears at St. Martin the Bishop in winter, which is the 11th day of this instant November," 1718.

These instances are sufficient to show the sort of work done by these Commissioners. Nothing but reference to Mr. Orlebar Payne's carefully-compiled volumes would show the scale on which it was carried on. The animus with which it was done is openly avowed by the Commissioners themselves in a letter addressed to the Lords of the Treasury. A plan had been proposed to them by the Treasury, which they say "sets the Roman Catholic interest very near in as good a condition as before the Rebellion: whereas, if they are divested of their estates, and Protestants succeed, the Roman Catholic interest in those northern counties must be entirely ruined." The Commissioners did not fully succeed in accomplishing their benevolent intention of " entirely ruining the Roman Catholic interest " in the northern counties, but they did a great deal towards it. The present state of Lancashire, where the Catholic religion has passed through many trials since then, is enough to show that they did not altogether succeed ; but they broke the strength of the northern Catholics in a way that has been felt ever since. It will be remembered that the estates of those Protestants only were interfered with who had taken actual part in the rebellion. Not so with Catholics. The Act of Parliament required all Catholic estates to be registered, and in case of default gave one-third to the person suing, and forfeited the remainder to the King. How this registration would facilitate the execution of the law of William III., disabling any Catholic from inheriting lands, and making the Protestant next of kin the heir, is self-evident.

To strike the landed gentry was the most effectual way of exterminating the Catholic religion. There were very few priests in the country whose home was not in some gentleman's house. Even as late as 1787, when Bishop Gibson, the Vicar Apostolic of the North, went his rounds to give Confirmation, he records not only the names of the priests, but in another column those of the gentlemen in whose houses they lived. Any forfeiture or confiscation of an estate meant one place less where a priest could find shelter. To have shut up all such Catholic houses would have been to have made priests houseless, and the Providence of God prevented the formidable machinery that was brought into play from effecting the extinction of religion by the total destruction of the homes where it found refuge. Be it ever remembered, to the eternal glory of the laity of England, that the Catholic faith has been kept alive in the land by their courage, which enabled priests to exercise their devoted self-sacrifice in behalf of their persecuted flock. The laity risked, and often suffered severe penalties, with heroic constancy ; but their numbers were thinned by the dying out of Catholic branches of their families, and alas.! subsequently, by loss of the faith for which they had suffered so much and so long.

CHAPTER II.

THE EIGHTEENTH CENTURY.

THE retrospect in which we are engaged into the times out of which we have emerged has brought us to the miserable eighteenth century, and one of the saddest parts of its sad story is to watch the disappearance of one Catholic family after another. In 1669 Canon Agretti reported to the Pope, "The Church has lost one family of consideration, and is about to lose another; for the Marquess of Worcester is dead, and his son, the new marquess, is a Protestant; and the Marquess of Winchester, whose son is a Protestant, is very old. It is believed that the Marquess of Worcester professed heresy for his own ends, and would not die except in the Catholic faith, as he had told several of his friends. Many act in this way to avoid injuring their temporal prospects."

"Their temporal prospects" were black enough. In Charles II.'s time one Act of Parliament disabled all Catholics from being "officers civil or military, from receiving salary or wages by any grant from the Crown, from having a command or place of trust in this kingdom, or in the navy, or the king's household." By the same Act, "all persons not bred up from their infancy in the Popish religion, and professing themselves Popish recusants, were disabled to bear any office in Church and State; their children educated in the Popish religion likewise disabled till reconciled to the Church of England, and qualified by taking the oaths of allegiance and supremacy and receiving the sacrament."

Another Act in the same reign was directed specially against members of the two Houses of Parliament. "Every peer of England and Ireland being twenty-one years of age, and every member of the House of Commons, who shall not take the oaths of allegiance and supremacy and the declaration against Transubstantiation and the Invocation of the Virgin Mary, was adjudged a Popish recusant convict, and was disabled to sit in

Parliament or vote by proxy in the House of Peers; to sue in any court; to be guardian, executor, or administrator; to take any legacy or deed of gift; and to forfeit £500 for every offence to him that will sue for the same."

It is not to be wondered at that such legislation led many men to act against their conscience. Fathers, heads of families, conformed, took these iniquitous oaths and declarations, and preserved their properties at the cost of their religion. They became what were called by their fellow-Catholics " schismatics," and men of all ranks so behaved. In Elizabeth's time the wife could continue to be a Catholic, without bringing pains and penalties on her conforming husband, but James I. struck at her also, disabling every one whose wife was a Popish recusant convict from holding any public office in the commonwealth, and adjudging every married woman, three months after conviction for recusancy, to be committed to prison without bail, until she conform, unless her husband will pay to the King £10 a month, or yield him a third part of his lands. There was no escape left open. A man's servants, even his children of nine years old, must repair to church once a month to save him from penalties, and that although he might himself have conformed. The persistent pressure of one Act after another, from the 35th of Elizabeth which forbade the Papist to go five miles from his home without a license from two Justices, down to William and Mary's prohibition to keep a horse above £5 in value—all the penal statutes, in fact, where each seemed to do all that law could do, and where another and yet another Act of Parliament found matter by which the persecution might be made more galling—in these are the excuses, if any excuses are possible, for numerous apostasies. Exterior conformity to escape penalties made England Protestant. All glory to the noble constancy of those who bore the pressure in spite of the example of their neighbours who yielded.

We must spend a few minutes in the unwelcome task of examining losses. Henry Somerset, the third Marquess of Worcester, of whose conformity Agretti has told us, came to the title in 1667, and after filling offices of the highest distinction, was in 1682 created Duke of Beaufort. His family motto was *Mutare vel timere sperno*, a motto that suited his father rather than himself.

John Paulet, the old Marquess of Winchester, mentioned by Agretti, was the patron and friend of the Jesuit Martyr, the

Ven. Peter Wright, who lived in his house as his chaplain. He died in 1675, and his conforming son, the sixth marquess, was created in 1689 Duke of Bolton.

It was therefore in the latter part of the seventeenth century that Catholics lost such support and help as could be given by these two marquesses. The promotion of each to higher honours might be held out to Catholic peers as a bait to show them to what they might aspire if they would sacrifice their religion.

Since the end of the seventeenth century the English Catholics have lost by extinction the titles of Marquess of Powis, Earls Rivers, Castlehaven, St. Albans, and Traquair, Viscount Fauconberg, Viscount Montague, Lord Aston of Tixall, Lord Langdale of Holme, and Lord Eure of Wilton. The Barony of Morley and Monteagle is in abeyance. Viscount Molyneux of Maryborough, Lords Abergavenny, Waldegrave, Windsor of Bradenham, and Brudenal of Stanton were Catholics; not so the Earls of Sefton, Abergavenny, Waldegrave, Plymouth, and Cardigan who represent them now. The Ropers Lords Teynham are no longer Catholics. The Earldoms of Rutland and of Salisbury have had Catholic holders, and the united Earldoms of Shrewsbury, Waterford, and Wexford, have lately passed to a Protestant branch of the Talbots. Other titles have been lost by attainder. Lord Widdrington of Blankney was attainted after the '15. The Earl of Derwentwater was not attainted only, but executed, and the large Derwentwater estates were given to Greenwich Hospital. The Earldom of Newburgh has passed to the Giustiniani. All these losses do not belong to the eighteenth century, but most of them do.

As for Lord Derwentwater, we learn from Father George Pippard, S.J., who attended him in the Tower, that on the Monday before he died, his life was offered him if he would change his religion. "He told it to me," says the martyr's confessor, "with the greatest transport of joy, and that having refused his life on such terms, he hoped it was not now making a virtue of necessity—that had he a thousand lives, he would sooner part with them than renounce his faith,—and with tears of joy in his eyes, he humbly thanked God for giving him this opportunity of testifying his love for Him." When the anniversary of Lord Derwentwater's death came round, Bishop Giffard wrote to the Countess that she was to "lift up her thoughts to Heaven and behold there the person she loved most on earth at the height of all glory and happiness." His death, he said, was "a grace not only wonderful for its operations in him, but also for the great and sensible effects it had on many others. How many converts did it bring into the Church? How many tepid and cold Christians did it awaken and animate with resolutions of a new life? How many, moved by his example, have turned their hearts wholly to God? These blessed effects both I," said the Bishop, "and many others have been witnesses of; but what is most comfortable to your ladyship is that your dear lord is raised to so great a degree of happiness and glory, that all the affections and wishes of a most loving wife can desire nothing beyond what he is now possessed of." It would be well if all our losses had been as honourable to us as this.

With Lord Derwentwater suffered William Viscount Kenmure, a Scottish peer. Another Scottish title that disappeared at this time by attainder was that of the Earl of Nithsdale. William, the fifth earl, has been made famous by the heroic conduct of his wife, Winefred, daughter of the Marquess of Powis. He had really been reprieved with the Earl of Cornwath and Lords Widdrington and Nairn, but it was not known, and on the night before the day fixed for his execution, he escaped from the Tower through the brave contrivance of Lady Nithsdale. The whole story was told by her afterwards, in a letter to her sister, Lady Lucy Herbert, the Superioress of the English Augustinian Nuns at Bruges; and the late Lord Herries, his lineal descendant, caused it to be accurately printed in the noble family record called *The Book of Carlaverock*. Lady Nithsdale's letter had often been printed before, but in a modernized form. No mere extracts would do it justice, and it is too long for insertion in this place.

In the list of noble families that have ceased to be Catholic, even in our own times, mention has been made of the Earldom of Shrewsbury. In Earl John's time there were at once nine Catholics alive who were in the entail, and yet Bertram, the last Catholic Earl, was the only one who lived to succeed him. The havoc done amongst Catholics of the middle and working classes by the change that befel the great families on which they depended, was of course immense. They were dispersed or gradually fell away from the faith in consequence of the closing of domestic chapels and therefore of the missions attached to them. Within very recent times there were many estates in various parts of the country where the tenants of the farms were almost all Catholics. There are very few such places now.

What has been said of the injury done to the poorer class of Catholics by the loss of their old Catholic landlords is of course not confined to noble families only. The extinction of wealthy Catholic landowners' families, or their ceasing to be Catholic, has happened far too often for enumeration. The Gascoignes are gone, and the Inglebys, the Sheldons, the Fortescues, and now the Turvilles, the Giffords, the Fermors, the Cliftons, the Fairfaxes, the Heneages, the Swinburnes, the Curzons, the Ropers—to content oneself with names that rise up almost spontaneously. And some that happily we still retain have been saved to us almost by miracle. Thus the title of Lord Beaumont for a short time ceased to be Catholic; and so, more than once in its history, has one that now could ill be spared, that of the Duke of Norfolk. The losses of one kind and another, in the sad years as they went by, are too sad to think about. It will be better for us to return to the records of persecution.

We have seen how Bishop Giffard had been various times in prison, including two years in Newgate, and how in six months he had to change his lodging fourteen times. "The continual fears and alarms we are under," he said, "is something worse than Newgate." The following example of arrests will serve to illustrate the early part of the eighteenth century. The amount of the bail required is remarkable.

In the Diary of Narcissus Luttrell, under the date Sept. 26, 1706, we learn that "information being given of several priests lurking about this city [London], the messengers at the close of last week seized near Red Lion Square three of them, viz., Giffard, Martin, and Matthews. The last is committed to Newgate, but the others were admitted to bail, each in £1,000, and two sureties in £500 a piece."

A little later on in the century, the Internuncio at Brussels wrote to Propaganda, that, in 1733, Bishop Williams, O.P., Vicar Apostolic of the Northern District, was "actually obliged to fly to remote places, to escape prison and torture, as the pseudo-Archbishop of York [Lancelot Blackburn] had issued a warrant for his capture, on account of his having made a conversion, which caused a great noise, of a Protestant minister, who, instructed by Bishop Williams, nobly resigned his rich prebend and publicly declared himself a Catholic."

A little later still, Bishop York, Coadjutor in the Western District, wrote in 1747 to Propaganda, "We are compelled to fly from house to house, and from city to city." Bishop Pritchard, O.S.F., the Vicar Apostolic, was sick. "I, his unworthy coadjutor," says Bishop York, "have been for eighteen months and more a fugitive from my ordinary residence, and as yet have no fixed abode."

About the same time we meet with the following account of a search in the house of a noble Catholic lady in the south of England. The date is December, 1745. "Last Sunday, several gentlemen of the Commission of the Peace for the county of Surrey, surrounded the house of Lady Petre at Lower Cheam a little before daybreak, and having got admittance partly by force, proceeded to search the same, but found only two pair of pistols, and a man concealed between the ceiling of the garret and the rafters, who had only a shirt, nightgown, and nightcap on. Upon examination he appeared to have been born at Tickhill in Yorkshire, and brought up a Popish priest near Antwerp. He prevaricated much; said his name was Joseph Morgan, whereas it appears to be Morgan Hansbie, and that he had officiated as priest in the family where he was taken for many years. They brought him about noon to Croydon. The occasion of this search, which was contrived and executed with the utmost secrecy, was owing to the great uneasiness of the inhabitants of all the adjacent villages, who firmly believed that great numbers of men, horse, and arms were concealed there in subterraneous passages."

Father Morgan Hansbie, O.P., was by birth a gentleman, as so many of the priests were in the persecuting times. He and his brother and sister were all registered in 1715, as having an income from land. The hiding-place in the garret was a poor one, into which the poor priest hurried when suddenly awakened by the noise of the magistrates' forcible entry. Most Catholic houses had formerly at least been provided with safer hiding-places. If Father Hansbie prevaricated about his name, it is not to be wondered at, for there was hardly a priest in England who was not passing under an *alias*. Bishop Challoner was sometimes called Willard; Gilbert Talbot, a Jesuit Father, who was really the thirteenth Earl of Shrewsbury, had for his *alias* the name of Grey.

Ten years before the arrest of Father Hansbie, we have the following account in the *Gentleman's Magazine* for February,

1735: "Sunday 23. About eleven o'clock, the Peace Officers going their rounds to the public-houses, to prevent disorderly smoking and tippling in time of Divine Service, discovered a private Mass-house at a little ale-house at the back of Shoreditch, where nearly a hundred people had got together in a garret, most of them miserably poor and ragged, and upon examination appeared to be Irish. Some few were well dressed, and several Mass-books were found with them. The priest made his escape out of a back door, leaving the rest to shift for themselves, whereupon some got out of a trap-door, and others, after giving an account of their names and places of abode, were let quietly depart. Notwithstanding, a great many met in the evening at the same place, declaring that Mass should be said there."

The tradition in the house of the Vicars Apostolic in London was that Bishop Challoner used to meet a number of Catholics on Sunday evening at a public-house called "The Ship," near the Turnstile leading into Lincoln's Inn Fields, and sitting there with a pot of beer on a little table before him, as a pretext for being there, he would preach to the Catholics present. The little table, marked with circles by the pewter pots, is preserved to our time. It is said that the floor was partly moveable, so that people in two stories could hear the preacher at the same time.

Having introduced the name of Dr. Challoner, we may take from his Life[1] the narrative of the last prosecutions brought against Catholic priests on account of their exercise of spiritual functions. In 1765 an informer named William Payne had succeeded in obtaining admission for several Sundays to chapels where Mass was said. "By commending the elegance of the sermons of the preachers, and the decency and devotion with which others assisted at the altar, he had from some unthinking Catholics fished out the names of most of the clergy: he had dogged them from the chapels to their own houses: he had, in like manner, discovered the names and habitations of several persons of the respective congregations; he had also, some time before, applied to Dr. Challoner himself for instruction in the principles of the Catholic Faith, hypocritically pretending that he was desirous of being admitted into the communion of the

---

[1] *The Life of the Venerable and Right Reverend Richard Challoner.* By Mr. James Barnard. London, 1784, pp. 156—195. The Very Reverend James Barnard was Bishop Challoner's Vicar General. His book is very disappointing.

Catholic Church; and when his diabolical scheme was ripe for execution, he engaged some others to join him in his attempt." This was, of course, that he might have witnesses to produce in court.

Payne's first application was to Lord Mayor Stephenson[1] for warrants, and being refused, he next applied to the Bishop of London, begging him to urge the Lord Mayor to grant them. Fortunately, Lord Mayor Stephenson could speak from personal knowledge of several Catholics, as well as of some priests, so he wrote such reasons to the Bishop for not disturbing them, that he was pacified. He then wrote to the Catholics accused, saying that though he saw no reason for putting the penal laws in execution, yet while they were unrepealed any common informer could set them in motion. He advised them therefore to compromise the matter with the officer to whom Payne had had recourse. Ten guineas were accordingly paid to the constable, as well as Payne's bill of costs.

As might be expected, this only made the informer more eager, and led him to present two bills of indictment to the grand jury at the Old Bailey; and, though with difficulty, he obtained warrants from the court for the arrest of the two persons indicted. This was soon followed by the arrest of several of the clergy, who were dragged from the altars, and kept in custody till they were bailed, the informer interposing every difficulty to their finding bail. This lasted from 1765 to 1778, for the first seven years of which time Dr. Challoner rarely passed a week without hearing of some step or other taken by Payne.

It is hard to see how this persistent persecution was worth the informer's while. He obtained a single conviction, and only on that occasion succeeded in making the £100 reward his own. One cannot but believe that he levied blackmail on the Catholics, who probably bought him off, in the way in which they were obliged in Elizabeth's time to bribe pursuivants.

The one case in which Payne succeeded was that of John Baptist Molony, a Franciscan Father, "who was taken up for exercising his functions in Kent Street, contrary to law, was convicted on the 23rd of August, 1767, and sentenced to perpetual imprisonment." This good priest was imprisoned in the New Gaol, Southwark, his only crime being the administration of the sacraments to a sick man. He was afterwards removed

[1] Sir William Stephenson was Lord Mayor of London in 1765.

to the King's Bench, and after four years' imprisonment, he was banished from England for life.

Some time after this, the Bishop himself, four priests, and a schoolmaster were indicted, and released on bail. For some reason or other, they were not put on their trial, but four other priests were tried and acquitted. One of these was the Rev. James Webb, whose trial before Lord Chief Justice Mansfield at Westminster on the 25th of June, 1768, practically repealed the Act of Parliament and put an end to these prosecutions.

The counsel for the priest objected that, as the Act of William III. says, "Whosoever shall apprehend a Popish Bishop, priest, or Jesuit, and convict him of saying Mass," it was necessary first to prove that the person indicted was a priest, and secondly to prove that he had said Mass. The counsel for the informer very naturally replied that this could not be the intent of the Legislature, as if such were the meaning of the statute, it would be impossible to prove any man a priest. The Chief Justice ruled, in favour of the priest, that proof of both was necessary, and said that after Molony's conviction in Surrey, the twelve Judges had consulted on the point and agreed in their opinion that the accused person must first be proved to be a priest; and their unanimous interpretation of the law was, that evidence against any one for having said Mass would not convict him of being a priest.

Payne had sworn that he had heard Webb say Mass; and his proof was that he saw him dressed up in vestments with a cross upon his back; that he, the informer, had looked over a coalheaver's shoulder, who had a prayer-book with the Mass in Latin and English; that he had often been at the Ambassadors' chapels and seen priests say Mass there; and that James Webb did the same as they did. In reply, besides other objections to this evidence, the priest's counsel told this story, which the Judge accepted as conclusive. "In the reign of Queen Elizabeth there was a noted lawyer whose name was Plowden, and being a Roman Catholic he had many enemies in the country where he lived, and you must know there was a Payne amongst them. What did they do, but contrive to have Mass said, so that Mr. Plowden might be present. There was a priest, altar, vestments, candles, and everything necessary. Mr. Plowden very innocently went to hear Mass. It was scarce over but he was arrested with a warrant for hearing Mass, and was actually tried for it. The evidence appeared against him and swore positively that they saw Mr. Plowden hear Mass. At last the priest himself appeared against him, and swore that Mr. Plowden heard Mass, for that he himself had said Mass, and that he saw Mr. Plowden there. 'Pray,' says Mr. Plowden, 'let me ask you a question. Are you a priest?' 'No,' replied the other. 'Oh, then,' said Mr. Plowden, 'the case is altered: no priest, no Mass.'"

The other side might well plead, "We shall be obliged to go abroad into their Colleges and Seminaries, and even to the very place where they were ordained, and to the Bishop that ordained them, and perhaps to Rome, and even to the Pope himself, before we can prove them to be priests." The Chief Justice summed up strongly in favour of the prisoner, the jury acquitted him, and though as late as February 27, 1771, Bishop Talbot was put on his trial for exercising the function of a Popish Bishop, neither priest nor Bishop has ever since been found guilty under the penal Acts. In revenge for the part thus taken by him in practically changing the law, Lord Chief Justice Mansfield's house was one of those destroyed by the rioters under Lord George Gordon.

Before saying anything of these historic riots and of the relaxation of the penal laws that provoked them, it may be well to give a few minutes' attention to Bishop Challoner himself personally, and to his friend Alban Butler. They were our greatest men in the wretched eighteenth century, and they have done more than any of their contemporaries in preserving the faith amongst men of their own generation, and in promoting conversions to the Church. Challoner's books were exactly suited to his time and are not unsuited to ours, and Alban Butler's *Lives of the Saints* has not yet been, and is not likely to be, superseded.

Richard Challoner was sent to the English College at Douay in 1704, and left it in 1730. He was ordained priest in 1716; in 1712 he began to teach, and in the latter part of his time at College he was at once Vice-President, Prefect of Studies, Professor of Dogmatic Theology, and Confessor. In 1727 he took the degree of Doctor in Divinity. All this time devoted to study and to teaching fitted him for the literary work that awaited him in England. The list of his books would fill a page. They are remarkable in the first place for their painstaking accuracy, and next for a gentle unassuming persuasiveness, that was due as much to the writer's piety as to his learning. His books were the saving of Catholics who needed support and instruction, and they were well adapted to break down the absurd prejudices of Protestants as to the doctrines that the Church really teaches.

The Bishop who succeeded Dr. Buonaventure Giffard as Vicar Apostolic of the London District was Dr. Benjamin Petre, of Fidlers in Essex. In 1738 Douay College on the one side and Bishop Petre on the other engaged in a friendly rivalry, to obtain Dr. Challoner from the Holy See, the one as its President, the other as his coadjutor and successor. In the end Bishop Petre prevailed, and consecrated Dr. Challoner on the 29th of January, 1741. Bishop Petre survived till the end of 1758, and almost immediately after his death Bishop Challoner, falling sick, petitioned for and obtained as his coadjutor, with right of succession, the Hon. James Talbot, who was consecrated on the 24th of August, 1749. Dr. Challoner did not long survive the Lord George Gordon riots. He was buried at Milton in Berkshire, and the entry in the Parish Register runs thus: "Anno Domini 1781, January 22. Buried the Reverend Dr. Richard Challoner, a Popish priest, and Titular Bishop of London and Salisbury, a very pious and good man, of great learning and extensive abilities." The "Bishop of London and Salisbury" is evidently what remained on the Rector's mind after being told that he was Vicar Apostolic of London and Bishop of Debra.

Alban Butler, Challoner's fellow-professor at Douay, was the more learned man of the two. A story is told of him by his nephew, Charles Butler, as illustrating the exceedingly wide character of his knowledge. One day he attended a reception held by the Bishop of Arras. On being announced by the servant, the guests fell back on either side to allow him free passage to the Bishop. This however they did, thinking the person announced as M. l'Abbé Butler to be a well-known French priest of the name. Not recognizing the new-comer, they closed in again; and the Bishop, who knew his value, vexed that he should have an ungracious reception, took him by the arm, and led him round to the various groups who were conversing in the room, telling them there was no question they could put to the Abbé Butler that he would not be able to answer. A party of officers asked him about the trajectory of a cannon-ball; some young gentlemen asked him the classical name of the pear called *Bon chrétien*, respecting which he said that there were two opinions which he gave; and some ladies inquired what ladies' head-dresses were like in the fourteenth century, which he answered by referring them to the horned head-dresses on the tombs at Fontevrault that he had lately visited.

The modesty of the man was more remarkable even than his learning. When he had written his *Lives of the Saints*, he sent the manuscript to a friend for his advice, and on being recommended to publish it without the notes, he did so, though thus the first edition appeared without that portion of his work that had cost him the most labour and that possessed by far the greatest value. We are indebted for *The Memoirs of Missionary Priests*, the admirable book that has saved our Martyrs from oblivion, to Challoner and Alban Butler conjointly. The materials of the book published by Challoner were put together for him by Alban Butler, and they are now preserved at Oscott.

Challoner had the happiness of seeing the first beginnings of relaxation of the oppressive penal laws. The first address to the Crown that Catholics were permitted to make was presented by several Irish peers and about three hundred Commoners of substance and position in Ireland. It recounted that "there are a set of men, who instead of exercising any honest occupation in the commonwealth, make it their employment to pry into our miserable property, to drag us into the courts, and to compel us to confess on our oaths and under the penalties of perjury whether we have in any instance acquired a property in the smallest degree exceeding what the rigour of the law has admitted; and in such case the informers, without any other merit than that of their discovery, are invested (to the daily ruin of several innocent industrious families) not only with that surplus in which the law is exceeded, but with the whole body of the estate and interest so discovered: and it is our grief that this evil is likely to continue and increase, as informers have in this country almost worn off the infamy which in all ages and in all other countries has attended their character, and have grown into some repute by the frequency and success of their practices."

The Irish petition having been well received, an address was presented to George III. on the 31st of April, 1778, by the Earl of Surrey and the Lords Linton (afterwards seventh Earl of Traquair) and Petre, signed by ten of the English Catholic nobility and about two hundred of the principal gentry. The consequence was that an Act of Parliament was passed in the same year, "for relieving His Majesty's subjects professing the Popish religion from certain penalties and disabilities imposed on them by an Act of the 11th and 12th years of King William III." Hitherto no Catholic could take an oath of allegiance without the oath of supremacy and the declaration against Transubstantiation. The new Act imposed an oath of allegiance without any renunciation of Catholic doctrines. It renounced allegiance "unto the person taking upon himself the style and title of Prince of Wales in the lifetime of his father, and who since his death is said to have assumed the style and title of King of Great Britain by the name of Charles III." It rejected "as an un-Christian and impious position that it is lawful to murder any person or persons whatsoever for or under pretence of their being heretics; and also that un-Christian and impious principle that no faith is to be kept with heretics." And it declared that it is no article of faith, and it abjured "the opinion that princes excommunicated by the Pope and Council, or by any authority of the See of Rome, or by any authority whatsoever, may be deposed or murdered by their subjects;" and it renounced the belief that the Pope "hath or ought to have any temporal or civil jurisdiction, power, superiority, or pre-eminence directly or indirectly within this realm."

The Act was known as Sir George Savile's; and he was rewarded for it by the destruction of his house in the Lord George Gordon riots. In introducing the Bill he described the penalties on Catholics as "disgraceful not only to religion, but to humanity." By Sir George Savile's Act, the penalty of perpetual imprisonment on Popish priests and Popish schoolmasters was repealed, and Papists were rendered capable of inheriting and buying lands.

More than a year passed before the outburst came, prompted by Protestant bigotry, the growth of a couple of centuries, and by the usual reckless love of destruction that animates a mob. Lord George Gordon, a grandson of the last Catholic Duke of Gordon, was the President of the Protestant Association. He was simply a fanatic madman, and for a week he was at the head of a hundred thousand rioters in the capital of the kingdom. The first move was to present a monster petition to the House of Commons for the repeal of the small instalment of justice that had been accorded to the Catholics. It was said to have been signed by 120,000 names or marks. This was presented on Friday the 2nd of June, 1780, by the Protestant rioters in full force.

From Palace Yard, whither they had accompanied the petition with flags and bagpipes, a part of the mob in the evening went to the Sardinian Ambassador's chapel in Duke Street, Lincoln's Inn Fields. There they broke the chapel open and pulled down the altar, the communion-rails and seats, and carrying them into the street, set them on fire against the chapel doors. In about twenty minutes the chapel caught fire, and the mob would not suffer the engines to play on it till the Guards came. Several ringleaders were taken, but were soon rescued.

Another party broke open the Bavarian Ambassador's chapel in Warwick Street, Golden Square. The plate had been secured before their coming, but they naturally took possession of the alms-boxes. When they had partly demolished the chapel furniture, they were interrupted by the soldiers, who took thirteen into custody, several of whom had received bayonet wounds. The houses of the Bavarian and Sardinian Ambassadors had been broken into, and three of the rioters were taken in the latter. Great depredations were likewise committed in and about Moorfields. This was the first day's work, and was a mere prelude to what followed.

On Sunday, in the afternoon, a mob revisited the Sardinian chapel, destroyed the repairs that had been hastily made the day before, and were proceeding to pull down the walls, when the Guards from Somerset Barracks dispersed them.

On the same afternoon another body stripped the Catholic chapel in Ropemaker's Alley, Moorfields, and three Catholic houses, and then made a bonfire of the furniture. The *Political Magazine*, from which these details are taken, remarks on the burning of the crucifix, that "the most believing and pious Christians" had thought fit to burn our Lord in effigy.

The next day they took what they had left unburnt at Moorfields, and after carrying these pieces of wood to Lord George Gordon's house in Welbeck Street, they burnt them in the adjoining fields. Meanwhile the chapels in Virginia Lane, Wapping, and in Nightingale Lane, East Smithfield, were destroyed, a detachment of the Guards from the Tower looking on, as no magistrate called on them to interfere. Moorfields suffered still more. Not only the chapel, but the school, and the houses of Catholics were destroyed, everything being burnt that would burn, even the roofs. The schoolmaster's house was pulled down in an hour, and then some thousands went to a school in Charles Square, Hoxton, and wrecked it. Sir George Savile's was amongst the private houses destroyed on this day.

By Tuesday, June 6th, terror had become general. Every one who had occasion to go into the streets put on a blue cockade, for there was no safety without "this badge of riot." More soldiers were called into London, and the troops were stationed in St. James' Park, the Tower, and in the streets leading to the Houses of Parliament, but they had no orders to act. The first act of violence committed by the rioters this day was the burning of Newgate and the release of all the felons there confined. They then went down Snow Hill and stopped at Mr. Langdale's at Holborn Bridge. He was a Catholic who had a large distillery, and on the threat of the mob to destroy his house and property, spirits were brought out in tubs and pails, and all helped themselves that chose to do so. The rioters then divided into various parties. One set went up Holborn Hill through Hatton Garden to Clerkenwell New Prison, where they made a complete gaol-delivery. A second party broke into Sir John Fielding's house in Bow Street, and wrecked and burnt the furniture. Others went to attack the Catholics in Devonshire Street, Red Lion Square, which was known to be the place where Bishop Challoner usually lived.

The day following, every house hung out a blue flag, and the watchword of the insurgents, "No Popery," was written up everywhere. About six in the evening great bodies of men assembled in different quarters of the town. One strong party went over Blackfriars Bridge, first stopping some time at Bridewell Hospital, and on arriving at the King's Bench Prison, where they were joined by the Borough rioters, they set fire to the prison. Another formidable body broke into the Fleet Prison and set it on fire. A third strong body of the insurgents went again to Mr. Langdale's at Holborn Bridge, where since the evening before they had had spirits brought out to them as they chose. About seven in the evening they forced their way into the still-house, and rolled out the casks of spirits, of which numbers of them drank immoderately. Whilst this was going on, others were plundering the house. Everything that would burn they piled up opposite to St. Andrew's Church, and made an immense bonfire. About nine at night the still-house took fire, and the spirits that remained blazed with great fury. The flames soon reached the backs of the houses in Field Lane, several of which were burned down. By ten o'clock Mr. Langdale's dwelling-house began to burn, and it, with two houses on one side and one on the other, was entirely consumed.

At the same time another house on Holborn Hill, just above Fetter Lane, belonging to Mr. Langdale's son, was destroyed in like manner, with the distillery adjoining it. Casks of spirits were emptied into the street. The fire extended into Barnard's Inn, part of which was burned. The toll-houses on Blackfriars Bridge were also burned. Many private houses shared the same fate, and the Catholics were surprised to find that the ringleaders were furnished with lists of houses to be attacked and destroyed. In some cases Protestant neighbours offered Catholics shelter, in others they were afraid to do so; and the fear lest their turn might come next, of being driven with wife and children into the streets, homeless and friendless, involved every Catholic in the common misery. At length the Government issued a proclamation that the riot was to be suppressed by force. The prisons were already broken open and destroyed; the Bank, the public offices, and the houses of the Ministers were threatened, and the requisite measures were tardily taken to save the rest of London. Five and twenty thousand soldiers attacked the mob in various directions, and in the morning five hundred killed and wounded rioters were lying in the streets. Fifty-nine were afterwards condemned to death and twenty of them executed. The insane author of these calamities, Lord George Gordon, died in Newgate, professing himself to be a Jew. At last the cry of "No Popery" was hushed.

Bishop Challoner was aroused from his sleep on the night of Friday, the 2nd of June, by the news of the attack on the Sardinian Chapel, and he was with difficulty induced to leave his house. On the following day he was taken to Finchley, to the country-house of Mr. William Mawhood,[1] a leading man amongst the London Catholics. Mawhood was a woollen merchant and army clothier, who had a large house and place of business in West Smithfield. On the Monday and the Tuesday of the riots, this house was visited and the rioters

---

[1] *Biographical Dictionary.* By Joseph Gillow, Esq. Art. "Challoner." Three volumes of this most useful Dictionary have appeared. When the work is complete, it will be a perfect storehouse of English Catholic history in modern times.

threatened to destroy it, and the owner's house at Finchley also On Wednesday, the Bishop spent an hour in prayer while the coach was at the door, which was prepared to carry him to a place of greater security. He then told the family that "he who dwells in the help of the Most High shall abide under the protection of the God of Heaven," and he assured Mr. Mawhood that he was certain that no harm would happen either to his country-house or his town-house. The Bishop's prediction was exactly verified.

The sequel showed how signally times were changed. Property destroyed in a riot must be made good by the county. Not very many years before, Catholics would never have dreamed of hoping that restitution might be made to them for their losses. They were now told that they had taken the oath of allegiance to the King and were under the protection of the laws, like all other subjects. Compensation was therefore made to them, as well as to the Protestants, whose property had been destroyed by the mob. Instead of hurting the Catholics, in the long run the riots helped them forward towards their final emancipation.

CHAPTER III.

CATHOLIC EMANCIPATION.

THE measure of toleration granted in 1778, which had aroused all the Protestant fury of the Lord George Gordon riots, was very limited, but the Catholics were quite right to accept it as sure to lead to more. Lord North had said to Mr. William Sheldon, through whose hands all negotiation between Government and the Catholics passed at that time, "At first be satisfied with anything. The great object is to make a breach in the wall of intolerance. Do this, and if you act with prudence, and are not too much in a hurry, you will certainly get on." The wisdom of this advice was shown by the speedy passing of the Toleration Act in 1791, which was a very substantial instalment of our civil rights.

It may well be imagined that some Catholics were over-eager to obtain these concessions. The relaxation of the penal laws had naturally produced the effect of causing Catholics to fear and dread their revival. As long as they were on the statute-book, this might happen at any time. The discussion on the repeal of these laws, the hesitation of their friends, the opposition of their enemies, induced them to make a bid to Protestants for their liberty. Not content with denying the false charges that were made against the teaching of the Church, and Protestant misrepresentations of Catholic practice, in their eagerness to obtain the object in view, some Catholics went too far in their desire to please Protestants. The position of the Vicars Apostolic was thus made extremely difficult.

In 1782, at a meeting of Catholics, five laymen belonging to old and highly respected Catholic families were appointed a Committee for five years to promote the political interests of Catholics. The Vicars Apostolic at the time were Bishop James Talbot in London, and his brother, Bishop Thomas Talbot, in the Midland District, brothers of George 14th Earl of Shrewsbury; in the Western District Bishop Charles Walmesley, the mathematician; in the Northern Bishop Matthew Gibson. The gravity of the collision between the Committee and the Bishops may be judged by the fact that when Bishop Matthew Gibson died in 1790, his brother and successor in the Episcopate, Bishop William Gibson, wrote to Propaganda that his death had been hastened by grief at the attempts made by many to diminish or destroy the Pope's authority and jurisdiction in England.

The Committee began by urging what would have been a very reasonable request if it had been put forward on good motives. They asked that an English Hierarchy should be substituted for our ecclesiastical government by Vicars Apostolic. The avowed motive was based on ignorance of Canon Law, for it was "that the frequent recurrence to Rome for dispensations, and other ecclesiastical matters may cease." Bishops in ordinary stand in as much need of faculties from the Holy See as Vicars Apostolic, in order to grant the dispensations of which the Committee speaks.

The appointment of this Committee had been for five years. Before that time had elapsed, it was remodelled and its number raised to ten, but its spirit did not change. The Committee of five had proposed, in 1786, as a doctrinal test, to be signed by all Catholics and presented to Parliament, a statement of Catholic principles with reference to God and the country, which statement was an anonymous tract, edited, with alterations, by the Reverend Joseph Berington. The London Vicar Apostolic wrote to his brother in the Midlands, "If such a test is necessary, they should have told us why, and asked the thing of us, instead of choosing for us." The opposition of the Bishops, aided by the learned Bishop Hay, a Scotch Vicar Apostolic, saved the English Catholics from committing themselves to this unauthorized "doctrinal test."

In the following year, 1787, the newly-formed Committee of ten laymen printed a circular that contained these words: "We beg leave to observe that the ecclesiastical government by Vicars Apostolic is by no means essential to our religion, and that it is not only contrary to the primitive practice of the Church, but is in direct opposition to the Statute of Præmunire and Provisors." Canon Flanagan, in his *History of the Church in England*, is deservedly severe on Catholics who appeal to the primitive from the present discipline of the Church, and shelter themselves behind persecuting statutes.

To strengthen the Committee and remove the general distrust felt by Catholics of the lower and middle classes, three clerical members were added to it in 1788, Bishop Charles Berington, Coadjutor to the Vicar Apostolic of the Midland District, the Reverend Joseph Wilks, and, besides these two who had always been favourable to their proceedings, Bishop James Talbot, the London Vicar Apostolic. Their object was to draw him over to their side; his, as he told Dr. Milner, was to restrain them by a formal protest. The Bishop's presence, however, was no check on the Committee.

A "Declaration and Protestation" was prepared by the Committee and was very largely signed by both clergy and laity throughout the country. Milner strove in vain to obtain a change in various expressions that were theologically inexact, as that "neither the Pope nor any prelate nor any priest can absolve us or any of us from, or dispense with, the obligation of any compact or oath whatsoever." "This," wrote Dr. Milner, "is protesting more than is strictly true."

The title, "A Protestation," given to this document, had an object. It was intended to break down the distinction between Catholics and their Protestant fellow-subjects by the adoption of the epithet "Protesting" for Catholics also, reserving the name of "Papist" for all who should hold what they protest against. The Relief Bill prepared by the Catholic Committee proposed that all Catholics who desired to benefit by its provisions should sign this declaration in a court of justice. "I, A. B., do hereby declare myself to be a Protesting Catholic Dissenter." And one of the clauses of the Bill provided that no child of a "Protesting Catholic" should be educated a "Papist." In spite of promises previously made that they would propose no new oath, the Committee attached to their Bill a form of oath, which amongst other things declared that no foreign prince or prelate hath or ought to have "any spiritual authority, power or jurisdiction whatsoever, that can directly or indirectly affect or interfere with the independence, sovereignty, laws or constitution of this kingdom, or with the civil or ecclesiastical government thereof, as by law established."

The Vicars Apostolic met at Hammersmith and wrote an Encyclical Letter to all the faithful of the four districts of England. "We think it necessary to notify to you that, having held a meeting on the 19th of October, 1789, after mature deliberation and previous discussions, we unanimously condemned the new form of an oath intended for the Catholics, published in Woodfall's *Register*, June 26, 1789, and declared it unlawful to be taken. We also declared that none of the faithful, clergy or laity, under our care, ought to take any oath, or subscribe to any new instrument, wherein the interests of religion are concerned, without the previous approbation of their respective Bishops." The Vicars Apostolic had with them in their meeting as counsellors two Bishops, the Coadjutors of two of their number, and two priests, one of whom was the famous John Milner, then in charge of the Winchester mission. His presence there is strongly indicative of the mind of the Vicars Apostolic on the subjects under discussion, for he was the true, unwearied, and ultimately successful champion of the Church's spiritual liberty during this long and painful controversy in the midst of the Catholics of England. The Hammersmith Encyclical expressed in plain terms that view of the matters under discussion which was taken by Dr. Milner throughout. That he, and the English Vicars Apostolic, were in the right from the outset, is shown by the fact that the Bishops of Ireland and Scotland gave their adhesion to this Encyclical, and that it received the approbation of the Holy See.

Unhappily the Committee did not submit, and the colour of the cover of their publication gave its name to the unhappy Blue Book controversy. Their chief opponents among the clergy were the Reverend John Milner, who in 1803 became Vicar Apostolic of the Midland District, the Reverend William Pilling, O.S.F., and the Reverend Charles Plowden, a member of the Society of Jesus up to the time of its Suppression, and afterwards the holder of high office in the restored Society.

In the January of 1790 Bishop James Talbot died, and in May Bishop Matthew Gibson. The Committee seized the occasion to put forward the right which they pretended was inherent in the clergy and laity to elect their Bishop without reference to Rome. One of their number called the Vicars Apostolic "foreign emissaries, who preside in virtue of an authority delegated by a foreign prelate, who has no pretensions to exercise such an act of power." We were then apparently threatened with a schism resembling that of the Jansenists at Utrecht in those days or of the "Old Catholics" in Germany in our own; but though the larger number of laymen of rank and fortune sided at all events to some extent with the Committee, the clergy almost universally supported the Vicars Apostolic, who happily were unanimous, and the middle and lower classes of Catholics, with some portion of the more wealthy also, were staunch and firm.

Bishop Charles Berington, the Coadjutor of the Northern District, who was himself a member of the Committee, was regarded by it as the "elected" Bishop of London. Happily when Dr. John Douglas was appointed by the Holy See to succeed Bishop James Talbot, Bishop Charles Berington printed a letter to the London clergy, renouncing all claims on his part and calling on the other members of the Committee to submit themselves to Bishop Douglas.

This was dated November 4, 1790, and on the 5th of the following month Bishop William Gibson was consecrated by Bishop Walmesley, and a fortnight later Bishop Douglas by Bishop Gibson. It was significant that the two priests who assisted in the place of Bishops at the first of these consecrations were the Reverend Charles Plowden and the Reverend John Milner. This double consecration took place at Lulworth Castle, the owner of which place, Mr. Thomas Weld, was a steady supporter of the Bishops, and of the liberties of the Church. The three Bishops who were thus met together, signed an Encyclical, which renewed in the fullest manner the condemnation of the proposed oath. It exhorted Catholics to oppose the oath to the best of their power if it were introduced into Parliament. It condemned the term "Protesting Catholic Dissenters, given us in the Bill." And it said of some recent publications, that they were "schismatical, scandalous, inflammatory, and insulting to the Supreme Head of the Church, the Vicar of Jesus Christ."

Before publishing this Encyclical the Bishops made an effort to win over the Committee, and especially its Secretary, the learned and well-known Charles Butler. No good resulting from these charitable overtures, the Encyclical was published on the 19th of January, 1791. The Committee immediately issued a violent "Protest," declaring that "every clause, article, determination, matter, and thing therein respectively contained was arbitrary and unjust, full of misrepresentation, encroaching on our natural, civil, and religious rights, hostile to society and Government and the constitution and laws of the British Empire, derogatory from the allegiance we owe to the State and the settlement of the Crown:" and appealing "to all the

Catholic Churches in the universe, and especially to the first of Catholic Churches, the Apostolic See, rightly informed."

The Bill of the Committee, which proposed relief to the Protesting Catholic Dissenters and to no others, was at length read in Parliament. Dr. Milner, as the representative of the Bishops, circulated in the House a paper entitled, "Facts relating to the contest among the Roman Catholics." To this, in the course of the debate, Sir Archibald Macdonald, the Attorney General, called attention, saying that "one of the Catholic parties were as good subjects and as much entitled to favour as the other;" and Pitt exclaimed, "We have been deceived in the general outlines; and either the other party must be relieved or the Bill not pass." It is a comfort to be able to say that in the House of Lords the Archbishop of Canterbury and the Bishops of Salisbury and St. David's supported the relief of Catholics in ampler form than that provided by the Bill, and the last mentioned of these Anglican Prelates, Dr. Samuel Horsley, embodied in his speech all that Dr. Milner's pamphlet had urged.

The title of "Protesting Catholic Dissenters" was struck out of the Bill in the Commons; the proposed oath was discarded, and at the suggestion of Bishop Douglas, when the Bill was before the Lords, the Irish oath of 1778 was substituted for it. The Bill passed both Houses of Parliament *nemine dissentiente*, repealing the statutes of recusancy and various disabilities in favour of those taking the oath, and tolerating the schools and religious worship of Catholics. The double land-tax was never again enacted, but it was paid in many cases till 1831, when an Act was passed to relieve Catholics from it.

By this Act of 1791 all Catholics taking the oath of allegiance were exempted from persecution as recusants for not going to church,[1] for being Papists or reputed Papists, for hearing or saying Mass, for being present at, or performing any religious rite, or for being priests or deacons, religious or schoolmasters. The oaths and declarations of the Acts of William and Mary, Charles II. and George I. were no longer required, Catholics were no longer obliged to register their lands, they were allowed to live in London, Catholic peers were relieved from the penalties inflicted for coming into the King's presence without

---

[1] The Act contained the very singular provision that the law requiring every one to go to church on a Sunday, should be regarded as observed by those who went to a Catholic chapel.

having taken the declaration against transubstantiation, and barristers and attorneys were relieved from the oaths prescribed by the Act of William III. Catholic chapels were to be certified at Quarter Sessions, and it was only in chapels thus certified that religious worship was allowed under the Act, and no person could perform any religious rite therein, until his own name and description had been registered by the Clerk of the Peace. Disturbers of a Catholic congregation and persons "misusing a priest" were to be punished by a fine of £20. Priests who should take the oath imposed by the Act were exempted from serving on juries. The Catholic clergy are excluded from sitting in the House of Commons by the same Resolution of the House that excludes the clergy of the Established Church. Dissenting ministers are not excluded.

It was made unlawful to lock, bar, or bolt the chapel doors during service, from some lurking fear, apparently, that Catholics, whose concealments and disguises in time of persecution had simply been the defence of the weak against the strong, were a secret society that plotted against their neighbours and the State. Thus, also, a priest forfeited all benefit under the Act if he performed any ceremony of his religion, excepting in a certified chapel or in a private house with a congregation of less than five persons besides the household. The priest also lost the benefit of the Act if he should officiate in any place with a steeple or a bell, or at a funeral in any church or churchyard, or if he should wear the habit of his Order.

The action brought against the Redemptorist Fathers at Clapham for ringing their bells when the peal was first put up in their steeple, was not brought on the ground that it is illegal for Catholics to have church bells, but on the personal ground of the ringing being a nuisance to an individual, whose house adjoined the tower of the church. Many such peals have been erected since then in various places, and the traditional belief that Catholics were prohibited by law from ringing church bells by this time no doubt has died a natural death.

Officiating at the funerals of Catholics in the old churchyards of England, once Catholic and now in Protestant hands, has been recently permitted to priests by a Burial Act, which allows any religious service to be held in the churchyards in accordance with the religion professed in life by the person there buried. This clears away the second of the protests of the Toleration Act.

As to the third and last of them, when the late Mr. Scott Murray was High Sheriff of Bucks in 1852, his chaplain attended the opening of the Assizes at Aylesbury, wearing a cassock. Lord Campbell charged the Grand Jury against the presence of "a priest in the habit of his Order." Mr. Scott Murray replied in court that his chaplain "did not belong to any Order," meaning any Religious Order. Some months afterwards, Mr. Disraeli issued a proclamation against Catholic processions, which however recited the Emancipation Act as enacting "that no Roman Catholic Ecclesiastic, nor any member of any of the Religious Orders, communities, or societies of the Church of Rome, bound by monastic or religious vows, should exercise any of the rites of ceremonies of the Roman Catholic religion, or wear the habits of his Order, save within the usual places of worship of the Roman Catholic religion or in private houses." This proclamation took Father Ignatius Spencer by surprise. He was at the time at Southampton, giving a mission in his Passionist habit, and he returned to London scarcely recognizable in a slop suit of clothes, bought ready made.

The oath prescribed by the Act of 1791 was all that Catholic schoolmasters were henceforward required to take, but a provision was inserted that no Catholic could be the master of any school or college at Oxford or Cambridge, or of any royal foundation or other endowed school. It was also made illegal to found any Catholic school or college, all trusts for such a purpose being declared superstitious. The same section of the Act made it unlawful "to found or establish any Religious Order or Society of persons bound by monastic or religious vows." On the other hand, the benefit of the Act extended not only to priests and deacons, but to any one "entering or belonging to any ecclesiastical Order or community of the Church of Rome."

Father William Amherst, S.J., in his interesting history of Catholic Emancipation, calls attention to the difference between the provisions of the Relief Act and of the subsequent Act of Emancipation respecting our Religious Orders. The matter is of such grave consequence, that it will be well to give his words in full.

'The Act of 1791 made no distinction whatever, in the benefit which it gave, between the Secular and Regular clergy, who were then in England; and further, though by section xvii. it forbade an Order to be established, by section iii. it expressly allowed a man to "enter an

Order" and remain in England. The Act of 1829 contains, as is well known, clauses for providing for the gradual suppression of religious Orders; but the Act of 1829 goes further than the Act of 1791, and makes a most invidious distinction between the Secular and Regular clergy then in England: for "Jesuits," who had the distinguished honour of being specially named, and "members of other religious Orders, communities, or societies of the Church of Rome, bound by monastic or religious vows," are obliged by the Act to register themselves as such. And, moreover, whereas the Act of 1791 allowed a man to "enter an Order," that is, to take the vows of religion in an Order, the Act of 1829 made any man who should do so liable to banishment, and if he evaded that sentence, to transportation for life. In short, whereas by the Act of 1791, though no one could found or establish an Order, any one might enter an Order; by the Act of 1829 any one entering an Order is punished as a felon. So that the Act of 1829 virtually repealed a portion of the relief which had been granted by the Act of 1791.[1]

Father Amherst may well ask, "Are the Catholics of the United Kingdom generally aware that the great Emancipation Act deprived us of benefits which were granted when the repeal of the old penal laws began; that Religious Orders, before the law, have been since the Emancipation Act, and still are in a worse position than they were in between the years 1791 and 1829?"

The penalties under the Act are worth recounting as they are actually the law of the land. There was a heavy pecuniary penalty of £50 a month for neglect to register at the time the Act was passed. Regulars then abroad, if natural born subjects, were required to register within six months of their return, under the same penalty of £50 a month. Foreign religious coming into the kingdom without a Secretary of State's licence (to be in force for not more than six months), were liable to banishment. And—the most important of all the provisions for ourselves—all who shall admit or aid and abet admission into a Religious Order were, and are, guilty of a misdemeanour, punishable by fine and imprisonment. The person so entering an Order may be ordered into banishment from the United Kingdom for the term of his natural life, and if the order of banishment be disobeyed for three months, he can be transported for life.

[1] *The History of Catholic Emancipation, and the progress of the Catholic Church in the British Isles (chiefly in England) from 1771 to 1820.* By W. J. Amherst, S.J. Two vols. London: Kegan Paul and Co., 1886, vol. i. p. 181.

A few venerable veterans still survive of the religious who were registered under the Emancipation Act. That Act passed on the 13th of April, 1829, but its chief provisions were known throughout the kingdom before that date. In the month of March all those students of Stonyhurst who were desirous of entering the Society were forthwith admitted, though they continued their studies and were not sent to the Novitiate for a considerable interval. There were three in the classes of rhetoric, poetry, and syntax respectively, and one in rudiments. Of these ten, only one survives. The total number of Jesuits registered in England and Wales was 117, of whom 51 were priests, 56 scholastics, and 10 lay-brothers. Of those who were in the Society before Emancipation, there are still two surviving. May it be long before the three "registered Jesuits" pass away from the midst of us!

The late Father Randal Lythgoe was on the platform of a "No Popery" public meeting during the excitement that followed the establishment of the Hierarchy. He began his speech by stating that he was a priest and a Jesuit, and the announcement was met with loud cries of "Turn him out! Turn him out!" As soon as his voice could be heard, he turned the tide entirely in his favour by thumping his stick on the floor and saying, "I am a registered Jesuit, and I should like to see any two of you turn me out."

The generation of registered religious has very nearly passed away, and it is not a pleasant thought that the English Regulars of the present day are in this precarious position, that they are liable to banishment or penal servitude for life (the substitute for transportation), if ever an Attorney General should think well to put the law in motion against them. It is poor comfort to be told that, like the Titles Act, this clause of the Emancipation Act will never be put into execution. Who can say what may be done in a time of popular excitement? It is hardly to be expected that even at such a time a new penal law should pass, but a Government that would shrink from proposing a new law, might be urged to use one that still has its place on the statute-book. At any rate, it is mortifying to know that though at the end of the last century there came relief from every penalty in law against an Englishman who should enter a Religious Order, and that this immunity lasted for thirty-eight years without any evil consequence, a fresh penalty was imposed without rhyme or reason by an Act of Parliament that was supposed to have conferred upon us "Emancipation" from the pains and penalties previously inflicted on us for our religion.

Father Amherst thus comments on this state of the law:

> The attention of the legislature has several times been directed to the clauses of the Emancipation Act against Religious Orders. Some attempts have been made to obtain the repeal of those clauses, though the Catholics of England have never backed up the attempt as they ought to have done. A few years ago the subject was spoken of in the House of Commons, and Lord Beaconsfield, then in the Lower House, opposed the repeal of the clauses against Religious Orders, on the ground that though Jesuits and others were now perfectly harmless, yet they might become dangerous, and it might be as well to hold the clauses over them *in terrorem*. Passing by the expression of unjust suspicion, in which we may hope Lord Beaconsfield had too much sense to be sincere, it may fairly be said that, whatever may be the opinions of "the great Liberal party," the Conservatives of England, at least, might be well content to allow a man to enter a Religious Order in the year 1880, when William Pitt, the whole Bench of Bishops, the Houses of Lords and Commons unanimously, and King George III. himself were content to allow a man to do so in the year 1791.

This most important Toleration Act passed in June, 1791. In April, 1792, the Committee changed its name into "The Cisalpine Club," as a permanent protest against the "encroachments of the Court of Rome on the civil authority." The Club was a source of trouble and division for nearly thirty years, but later on it became perfectly harmless. The Reverend Joseph Wilks, one of the members added to the Committee in 1788, was suspended by Bishop Walmesley for refusing to read to the faithful the first Encyclical of the Vicars Apostolic and a Pastoral in the same sense issued by Bishop Walmesley, and for speaking publicly in defence of the condemned oath, at Bath, where he was missionary priest. The Cisalpine Club made his cause their own, and so did the Staffordshire clergy, thirteen priests in that county who unadvisedly wrote an "Appeal to the English Catholics." Happily all the clergy here mentioned, including the Reverend Joseph Wilks, retracted, "either in health or on their deathbeds."

Bishop Thomas Talbot, who had been absent from the last meeting of the Vicars Apostolic through illness, died in 1795, and Bishop Charles Berington succeeded to the Midland

Vicariate as Coadjutor. He had signed the second Blue Book issued by the Committee, and he had approved the oath that was condemned by the Vicars Apostolic. The Holy See required of him a retractation, as a condition without which the faculties granted to a Vicar Apostolic would not be conferred upon him. He hesitated and delayed for nearly three years, and when at last they were granted on his submission, he died before they reached his hands.

Much was yet wanting before Catholics could look on themselves as placed on an equality with their Protestant fellow-subjects. One provision of the Act of 1791 reads as if it were ironical, but of course it was looked upon as a serious concession. It enacted that Catholics might fill the offices of constable, churchwarden, and overseer of the poor, but by deputy only. They continued still to be debarred by law from every position in the State. They were excluded from Parliament, and even from the election franchise. They could not hold office under Government, nor were they eligible as members of corporations. No endowment for Catholic education was good in law. Catholic soldiers were obliged under penalties to attend the service of the Church of England, and the Toleration Act contained some restrictions even on the celebration of Catholic worship.

The attainment of Catholic Emancipation was a long and weary struggle. The poor old King thought that to give the royal assent to such an Act of Parliament would be a violation of his Coronation oath. The country was full of bigotry, the "No Popery" cry was general, petitions were numerously signed against any further concession to Catholics. An old woman, when asked to sign a petition against the Catholics, answered that "it was of no use, for the Scripture says that the Romans shall come and take away our place and nation;" and it seemed that better educated persons had the same fear that this would be the result of Catholic Emancipation. Catholics were not without friends in both Houses of Parliament, who introduced several Bills in their favour and spoke for them in many debates. One measure after another was rejected, and it seems as though English Catholics would never have obtained just treatment if Sir Robert Peel and the Duke of Wellington had not been obliged to change their policy, through fear of Ireland and of Daniel O'Connell.

Unfortunately the perfect union that had existed amongst

the English Bishops now came to an end. Three of the Vicars Apostolic were silent when it was proposed in Parliament to give the English Government a *Veto* on the appointment of our Bishops, and even, by accepting an endowment, to place our clergy under the control of the State. Bishop Milner was, after perhaps some hesitation in the matter, the only Bishop in England who held out against the *Veto*, but fortunately the Irish Bishops had confidence in him, made him their agent, and expressed themselves unmistakeably against the *Veto*. Many of the English Catholics, naturally, after what had gone before, took the opposite view. This divergence of opinion led to the expulsion of Bishop Milner[1] from the Select Committee of the "Catholic Board," another of Mr. Charles Butler's associations, where the Bishop's name had been placed without his knowledge, and to his exclusion from a meeting of the Vicars Apostolic held at Durham in 1813.

This is the main outline of that long and weary controversy; but Dr. Poynter, to whom the Catholic Board chiefly looked, was by no means invariably their supporter. He was a mild, peace-loving man, willing to yield when he thought it possible, and it is a happy thing for us that we had John Milner, with the Irish Bishops supporting him, to fight the battle of the Church. He at least spoke out fearlessly and honestly, and if he was blamed by the Holy See for a want of moderation in his expressions, and for needlessly irritating the feelings of others, he himself published that comment on his conduct, and on several occasions he amply apologized for any of his expressions that might have given offence, characteristically adding that he did not thereby mean to retract any fact or reason that he had had occasion to allege.

The proposal that the Catholic clergy should receive a State endowment originated with Pitt, and was intended of course to subjugate the Irish priesthood. Unhappily in 1810 Bishop Poynter signed a resolution consenting to give the English Government the *Veto* and a certain amount of control over the Church. So did Bishop Collingridge, and soon afterwards Bishop Gibson and his Coadjutor. Every effort was made in vain to win over Bishop Milner by fair means and foul. On one occasion he was invited by the Duke of Buckingham to

---

[1] Mr. Bodenham of Rotherwas and Mr. Weld of Lulworth withdrew with Bishop Milner. The account given by Father Amherst, vol. ii. pp. 114—119, is most interesting.

Stowe, where to his surprise he found himself beset after dinner with pressure of all kinds to obtain his signature. Early in the morning he sallied forth by a window, found his way to the stable and saddled his horse, and then, riding down the avenue, he sang, *In exitu Israel de Ægypto.*

The Bill which was drawn up in accordance with the resolution of the Catholic Board, was introduced by Grattan in April, 1813. It contained six oaths. Among them was a long oath mixing up bad theology with civil allegiance, and another forbidding Catholic priests to correspond with foreign prelates. All priests were to take these oaths within six months under penalty of misdemeanour, and without any shadow of benefit. The Bill required that every "instrument from the See of Rome" should be delivered in the original to the Secretary of State, for the Government to judge whether there was anything in it "injurious to the safety of the kingdom or to the Protestant Establishment." The Bill, which was rightly called one of pains and penalties rather than of relief, was rejected on its third reading. During the progress of the Bill, an outcry was raised against Catholics that they were enemies of the Bible. On this, Charles Butler and other Catholic supporters of the Bill instituted a "Catholic Bible Society," and they induced Bishop Poynter to become its President. It was condemned by the Holy See in 1816.

An episode in the story that caused great excitement both in Ireland and England was the arrival of a letter from Mgr. Quarantotti, Secretary of the Propaganda, written in February, 1814, when the Pope and Cardinals were absent from Rome. It went by the name of Quarantotti's Rescript. It was addressed to Bishop Poynter, and said that if the oaths were to some extent changed, "the Catholics ought to receive with content and gratitude the law which was proposed last year for their emancipation."

The Irish Bishops at once sent Bishop Murray, then Coadjutor to the Archbishop of Dublin, and Bishop Milner, to the Pope, to obtain the recall of Quarantotti's Rescript. Pius VII. received them in Rome, which city he had entered in triumph on the 24th of May, after his release from captivity. Mgr. Quarantotti was blamed for writing the letter without authority from the Pope, and the matter was referred to Cardinal Litta, the newly-appointed Prefect of Propaganda. The Catholic Board sent its congratulations to the Pope on his return to Rome, thanking him for the Quarantotti Rescript, which they had received with unspeakable joy. The answer made to them was that, as it had been issued in the Pope's absence, the whole subject would be examined afresh.

In consequence of the escape of Napoleon from Elba, Pius VII. left Rome with most of the Cardinals, and went to Genoa, where he would be under the protection of the English fleet. Bishops Poynter and Milner went also to Genoa, and the English affairs were at once taken into consideration. On the 25th of April, 1815, the decision of His Holiness was given on three points. First of all, three forms of an oath were given, any one of which the Pope would allow. Secondly, if Catholic Emancipation were granted, the Pope would permit the list of candidates to a vacant bishopric to be presented to the Government, with power to expunge the name of any obnoxious persons, provided that sufficient choice was left to His Holiness. Thirdly, the examination of documents from Rome could "not even be made a subject of negotiation."

On the earnest remonstrance of the Irish Bishops, the Pope declared that this letter was not preceptive, and that it contained nothing more than a permission to submit to the Government the ordinary list of candidates presented to a vacant see, if the usual electors pleased so to do. This was in November, and in a subsequent letter in February, 1816, the Pope said that he had followed the rule laid down by Benedict XIV., that the nomination to bishoprics should never be given to princes who are not Catholics, that he had only permitted "a certain power of exclusion," and that it was greatly to be wished that, in the appointment of Bishops, the Pope should enjoy "that full and complete freedom which so peculiarly belongs to our supremacy, and that no lay power had any share whatever in a matter of so much moment."

The four Vicars Apostolic were now happily reunited, and they all signed a declaration that, "as official guardians of the Catholic Church, we deprecate the surrender of the nomination of Catholic Bishops to a Prince, who is by law the head of a different religious establishment: nor can we assent to the interruption of the free intercourse in ecclesiastical matters, which must subsist between the chief Bishop and the other Bishops, subordinate pastors of the Roman Catholic Church."

Probably out of respect for Pope Pius VII., this document

makes no mention of a *Veto*, but by the good Providence of God, Catholic Emancipation, when it came in 1829, was hampered by no such concession. Concordats with the Holy See are not to the taste of Englishmen. They may be slow to see what justice requires, but when they see it, they will grant it without making it the matter of a bargain. In the case of every Concordat, the Church has to give up some portion of her rights, in order to obtain the recognition of the rest.

Bishop Milner died on the 19th of April, 1826, and when Bishop Poynter heard of his death, he compared him to St. Jerome. That he could be gentle and tender, as well as bold and uncompromising, is shown by the fact that by prudence and patience he succeeded in the end in inducing the thirteen Staffordshire priests to retract. This was worthy of the Bishop who introduced amongst his clergy the devotion to the Sacred Heart of our Lord, and put up a stained glass window of our Lord disclosing His Sacred Heart, in the little chapel of his Seminary at Old Oscott. Not long before his death, he declared to Mr. Havard, the preacher at Bishop Poynter's funeral, his "unbounded veneration for the virtues, piety, and edifying character of Dr. Poynter, and said that he would give the universe to possess half his merits in the sight of God."

Bishop Poynter died on the 11th of December, 1827, leaving his coadjutor Bishop Bramston to succeed him. Thus neither Bishop Milner nor Bishop Poynter, who had laboured each in accordance with his lights for the emancipation of English Catholics, lived to see the measure passed that granted it. It came in 1829, and it was nearer at hand than it looked when, on the accession of George IV. two other Emancipation Bills were introduced, containing the unsatisfactory provisions of the *Veto* Bill of 1813, and, after passing the Commons by a small majority, were thrown out by the Lords.

Happily for us, when Bishop Milner was gone, it was not left to Cisalpine Clubs to make terms for us with Parliament. Catholic Emancipation was due simply to Ireland and to O'Connell, and our position would have been very different without them. We had many friends of both political parties to whom our lasting gratitude is due, and amongst them we may make special mention of Sydney Smith, the well-known Canon of St. Paul's, who answered the popular objections with not much respect for the Catholic religion, perhaps, but with his own singular clearness and wit. The Duke of Wellington and Sir Robert Peel were in power, pledged to resist Catholic relief; but, alarmed at the state of Ireland, they resigned, were at once recalled by the King, accepted office, and to the dismay of their Tory followers, introduced and speedily carried the Catholic Emancipation Act of 1829.

The oath it contained, which has but lately been swept away with other oaths, had to be taken to enable a member of either House of Parliament to sit and vote. After swearing allegiance to George IV. and promising to maintain the Protestant Act of Succession, it rejected the opinion that excommunicated princes may be murdered, declared that the Pope had no temporal or civil jurisdiction within this realm, promised to defend the settlement of property established by the laws, abjured any intention to subvert the present Church Establishment, and promised never, by the exercise of any privilege, to disturb or weaken the Protestant religion or Protestant government in the United Kingdom.

We have already seen that, in one important respect, in order we must suppose to make the Act more palatable to its opponents, a concession was made to Protestant prejudice by enacting the gradual suppression of the Jesuits and all other Religious Orders of men. Our Regulars are liable at the good pleasure of the Attorney General, to banishment, or finally to transportation for life. This Act, we must repeat, still remains a blot upon the statute-book.

The Act further contained a prohibition to Catholics, forbidding them to take the titles of sees or deaneries occupied by Protestant dignitaries. The Ecclesiastical Titles Act went further, and prohibited all titles taken from towns in the Queen's dominions, but its repeal has not repealed the prohibition of the Emancipation Act. With the exception of St. David's, which remains disguised under its Latin title of Menevia, our Bishops at the re-establishment of the Hierarchy in 1850 took no title that was at that time held by a Protestant Bishop; and Provostships were instituted in our Cathedral Chapters instead of Deaneries. But whatever confusion would be produced by a Catholic and Protestant Bishop holding the same title, has been since disregarded by the Protestants themselves, who have made in recent times a Protestant Bishop of Liverpool and of Nottingham, and of other towns which were taken as titles by Catholic Bishops in 1850.

Though Catholics have been permitted to leave money for the endowment of their worship or their education, Masses for the repose of the soul of the deceased testator are still held superstitious and void. But this is not the case in Ireland. Under an Act passed in 1832, Catholics are placed on the same footing as Protestant Dissenters in respect of their schools, places of religious worship, education and charities in Great Britain, and the property held therewith, and the persons employed therein. Under this Act some gifts may be legalized which were previously invalid, but the Act does not in any way modify the provisions of either of the Relief Acts of 1791 or 1829 as regards Religious Orders. In 1860 another Act was passed to enable Catholics to take the benefit of the general law relating to charities without, however, altering the law as regards superstitious uses or objects deemed against the policy of the law.

Another great grievance has only been very partially remedied even yet. Lord Hardwicke's Marriage Act, which had been passed to get rid of the frightful abuse of the Fleet marriages, recognized no marriages as valid which were not celebrated according to the rites of the Church of England. Bishop Poynter in 1823 presented to Parliament the very reasonable petition that "the Roman Catholics in England might be placed on the same footing as those in Ireland, with respect to the performance of the marriage ceremony." In this present year, 1892, we might well make the same petition against our most irksome and injurious position under the Nonconformist Marriage Act.

As under the old Marriage Acts Catholics could obtain civil validity for their marriages only by presenting themselves before the Protestant clergyman, it was lawful in conscience so to do, as he thus was to them, not a minister of religion, but an official of the State. It was, however, not illegal for Catholics to be married by their own priests only, but as such a marriage carried with it no civil consequences, the children of such marriages in the eye of the law were illegitimate. Naturally enough, such marriages were contracted by none but the poor, and it had the effect of making the children of the Irish Catholic poor, born in England, chargeable on the respective parishes where they were born, as illegitimate children, and therefore not removeable with their parents when they became paupers and were sent back to Ireland.

When the marriage law was altered for the benefit of Nonconformists, it was made felony for the priest to celebrate marriage without the presence of a Registrar, which presence is only legal in a duly registered building. The only exception is when the parties have already contracted a civil marriage in the Registrar's Office, in which case the religious ceremony may be afterwards performed by the priest. As, however, in England the Canon of the Council of Trent on clandestinity has never been published, the civil ceremony is a valid though illicit and sinful form of marriage, and unless an impediment existed which has subsequently been dispensed, the priest would not remarry those who are civilly married. The penalty of the law punishes what may be a necessary part of the priest's duty, for he may be called upon to marry persons who have been living as man and wife, one of whom may be dangerously ill and unable to go to church.

Another evil that the existing marriage law has brought with it is its expense. The amount of harm this has done to the Irish poor in England is beyond calculation. It is one of the reasons, and probably the most powerful reason, why they are so often married in the Protestant church. In many towns the clergy of the Church of England marry the poor for a very trifling fee. This temptation, accompanied by the negligence of all inquiry respecting the parties, has wrought incredible injury to the religion and morality of the poorest Irish in the towns. With the remembrance of Ireland in their minds, in which country, owing to the publication of the decree of the Council of Trent on clandestinity, such marriages are not valid in the sight of the Church, they live after having been married in the Protestant church in grave doubt whether they are truly man and wife, and thus they fall into a total neglect of their religious duties. On this subject more must be said in the sequel. Here it is enough to rank it amongst our legal grievances, a remedy for which we hope for in the coming legislation about marriage. The adequacy of this measure is being watched with the greatest anxiety by all who know and care for our poor.

The Emancipation Act makes no mention of our marriages or of superstitious uses, but it creates a grievance, which, like the outlawry of our religious men, is an insult to our religion. When throwing open the offices in the State that had been closed to Catholics, it excepted the Lord Chancellorships of England and Ireland and the Lord Lieutenancy of Ireland. The Chancellorship of Ireland is now open to, and has been held by, a Catholic, but the two other restrictions were supposed to remain. It is greatly to be regretted that a recent effort to remove this invidious reflection upon Catholics, should have been unsuccessful. It was with little consideration rejected by the House of Commons, and the protest, subsequently published by the Duke of Norfolk, was forcible and dignified.

Since the debate in Parliament it has, however, been maintained that the discussion was unnecessary, and that there is now really no restriction on the appointment of a Catholic to either office. The form of the prohibition was that an oath was required that Catholics could not conscientiously take. Catholics were not legally disqualified from holding the office, if only they would fulfil whatever conditions the law required. While the law required that an un-Catholic oath should be taken, they were thereby excluded; but now that the oaths have been swept away, it is said that there is nothing to prevent a Catholic from holding the Lord Chancellorship of England or the Irish Viceroyalty. If this is so, it is singular that it was not brought before Parliament when the matter was under discussion. We should have been saved from a needless slur on our religion, and Parliament from a display of bigoted feeling, which would have kept a gate closed against us, that was believed to be shut, though it was really open.

CHAPTER IV.

OUR COMPONENT PARTS.

WE may say that our own times, as distinguished from the preceding times that prepared the way for us, began when the first of the Catholic peers availed themselves of the Emancipation Act and took their seats in the House of Lords. *The Times* of the 29th of April, 1829, in a leading article, spoke thus of this event of the day before:

> The first overt operation of the Catholic Relief Bill took place yesterday in the Upper House of Parliament, when His Grace the Duke of Norfolk, with Lords Clifford and Dormer, stood up at the table, repeated audibly after the clerk the oath prescribed by the new Act of Parliament, received the congratulations of the Lord Chancellor and of many noble and distinguished peers—amongst whom were the Dukes of Sussex and Leinster, Earls Grey, Fitzwilliam, &c.,—and resumed in their persons, if it can be called a resumption, the hereditary seats of their illustrious ancestors, which no Catholic had been suffered to occupy for 148 years. This ceremonial, though in its outward form, as simple as any oath administered to a witness before a country magistrate, was to us an exhibition in the highest degree both animating and affecting. We saw in the persons of these three noblemen, whose chief title to notice of any kind was the cause of their unmerited obscurity and insignificance, . . . the representatives of six or seven millions of British subjects. . . . The Catholic peers were not introduced as in the case of new peers; but they presented the writs, and thus entered the House as ancient peers. The Duke of Norfolk had been in the habit of sending each session for his writ, which he received. Lords Dormer and Clifford sent for theirs for the first time this Session.

On the 1st of May three more Catholic peers took the oaths and their seats, namely, Lord Stafford, Lord Petre, and Lord Stourton. For some reason or other, the Earl of Shrewsbury and Lord Arundell of Wardour did not take their seats at the same time with the other Catholic peers. The Parliament was soon dissolved, and but one Catholic sat in the Lower House during the Session in which Catholic Emancipation had been passed. Mr. Robert Hurst, who was member for Horsham, one of the Duke of Norfolk's pocket boroughs, at once applied for the Chiltern Hundreds, and on the 4th of May the Duke's eldest son, Henry Charles, Earl of Surrey, was returned as the first Catholic member to the House of Commons. In July, 1830, he was returned for the next Parliament, and so were four other Catholics for English seats, Mr. Edward Blount for Steyning, Sir Thomas Clifford Constable for Hedon, the Hon. Henry Stafford Jerningham for Pontefract, and Mr. Philip Henry Howard of Corby for Carlisle. Amongst the Irish members about ten were Catholics. In the *Catholic Directory* of the present year there are the names of seventy-two Irish Catholic members, and five Catholics in the House represent English constituencies, one of whom is the Home Secretary.

It would seem that in 1829 there were but eight Catholic peers—one Duke and one Earl, the *premier* Duke indeed and the *premier* Earl, and six Barons. In 1630, to judge by a list[1] sent to Rome, for which I am indebted to the Reverend William Greaney of Birmingham, there were in all 22 Catholic peers, six Earls (there was no Duke of Norfolk), four Viscounts, and 12 Barons. At the present time we have in all 39 Catholic peers, namely, one Duke, two Marquesses, eleven Earls, three Viscounts, and 22 Barons, including Irish titles. Of the 22 Catholic nobles named in the list of 1630, but five[2] had representatives to take their seats as Catholics in 1829, namely, Lords Shrewsbury, Petre, Arundell of Wardour, Stafford, and Stourton. The increase at the present time is due to various causes,—to titles being called out of abeyance like those of Lord Mowbray, Lord Camoys, and Lord Vaux of Harrowden, to creations of new peerages as those of Lord Gerard and Lord Acton, and to the conversions of noblemen, as the Marquesses of Bute and Ripon, the Earls of Denbigh and Gainsborough, and several more in each of these classes.

[1] In 1630, according to the paper quoted above, the Catholic peers were: The Earls of Shrewsbury, Worcester, Rivers, Castlehaven, St. Alban's and Winchester, (the Earl of Arundel, Thomas, son of Ven. Philip, not being a Catholic); Viscounts Somerset, Savage, Montague and Dunbar; Barons Abergavenny, Windsor, Petre, Brudenell, Baltimore, Morley and Monteagle, Vaux of Harrowden, Arundell of Wardour, Eure, Stafford, Teynham, and Stourton. There were besides, Lord Herbert and Lord Tunbridge, sons respectively of the Earls of Worcester and St. Albans, and the eldest son of Viscount Fairfax was a Catholic. The Lord Dormer of that day was Earl of Carnarvon, whose name was not included in the list. There must have been other Irish Catholic peers besides Castlehaven, Somerset, and Savage, and other Scotch peers besides Dunbar.

[2] There were ten Scotch and Irish peers in 1829, so that the numbers are 18 then and 39 now.

The political portion of our history may now be closed, and in order to treat of other things concerning us besides our relation to the State, we must begin by going back a little in date. In 1773 the Society of Jesus was suppressed by Pope Clement XIV. That event, which was fatal to such undertakings as the Reductions in Paraguay, produced in the first instance very little impression on Catholics in England. The Jesuits, who were in the country at the time of the Suppression, were almost all of them stationed in the houses of gentlemen, which were the centres of missions, and there they continued. At that time the Bishops, in their reports to Propaganda of the state of their Districts, state that there were on the mission 121 Jesuits, 44 Benedictines, 37 Franciscans, 8 Dominicans, 7 Regulars of other Orders, and 175 Secular Priests, making in all 392 priests, of whom 137 were in the Northern District, 120 in that of London, 91 in the Midland, and 44 in the Western.

The list given by Brother Foley of the Jesuits in England at the Suppression in 1773 gives a somewhat larger number than the 121 enumerated by the Bishops. There were in all 130; and of the 127 places where they were then stationed, no less than 114 have since been given up by them. There are only 13 places where Jesuits then were, where they are now to be found. The English Vicars Apostolic treated the ex-Jesuits with the greatest kindness and consideration, and they were pleased to regard the College at Liège, the "Gentlemen of the Academy," as they were called, at first, and afterwards the same body when transferred to Stonyhurst, as representing the suppressed Society and as empowered to nominate to the old Jesuit missions. A number of secular priests were brought up in the College; and even after the time when some of the English ex-Jesuits, especially those of Stonyhurst, were in 1803 aggregated to the Jesuits, whose existence in White Russia was recognized by Pius VII., these secular priests who were bound by no religious vows, were treated in many respects as if they belonged to the Society. They were provided with Jesuit missions, and after death they shared in the suffrages of their religious brethren. In 1803 there were in England 33 Fathers associated with the Jesuits of White Russia, 34 ex-Jesuits, and 24 secular priests. At the restoration of the Society by Pope Pius VII. in 1814, there were 40 English Jesuit Fathers, 10 ex-Jesuits, and 21 auxiliary secular priests. Of these last, the Reverend Henry Campbell of Grafton Manor, who died in 1874, was the last survivor. It may be well to add, for purposes of comparison, that there are now 197 Jesuit Fathers at work in England, omitting all *in statu pupillari*, including 75 in Colleges, none of which in 1773 were in England. It follows that, if those in Colleges are omitted, there are 8 fewer Jesuits at work on the mission now than there were at the time of the Suppression.

The goodness of the English Vicars Apostolic to the members of the Suppressed Society was not confined to English soil. The Jesuits were expelled from the English College at St. Omers in 1762. They took refuge in Bruges, where Maria Teresa promised them a shelter. When the Suppression came nine years later, though Maria Teresa changed her mind and joined in the Suppression, the people of Bruges made a great effort to retain the English College under the care of the ex-Jesuits, to be preserved and managed in the same way in which the College of Liège was continued under the care of the Prince Bishop of that city. Letters were written to the English Bishops by the Bishop of Bruges, and the answers of the four Vicars Apostolic are now in the Archives of the town. All of them wrote, favouring the project, Bishop Challoner being particularly cordial ; but Maria Teresa's government would not permit it, and the College at Bruges was closed. The preparatory College, which had been at Watten, and had likewise been transferred to Bruges, also ceased to exist. The boys who had been at Bruges went to Liège, and the whole establishment, when driven away from that hospitable city by the French Revolution, found a new home in Stonyhurst, which was given to them in 1794 by Mr. Thomas Weld.

If any awkwardness subsequently arose with any of the Vicars Apostolic, it was caused by the fact that Pope Pius VII., while he was extremely anxious to restore the Society, was also most careful not to do anything that would be displeasing to the English Government, to which he was deeply indebted. He therefore required the strictest secresy to be observed as to the newly restored English Province of the Society, and it is not to be wondered at that three out of the four Vicars Apostolic should have refused to ordain the members of the College except as secular priests. As this would have involved taking the oath not to enter a Religious Order, it was an impossible condition for men who were looking forward in hope of the speedy restoration of the Society throughout the world, and were at that time lawfully associated with the remnants of the old Society that, with the knowledge of the Holy See, still existed in White Russia. The College, in 1778, when at Liège had been made a Pontifical College by a Brief that had been obtained from Pope Pius VI. by the Prince Bishop, and Bishop Milner had no difficulty in ordaining the members of the College, though Stonyhurst was not in the Midland District. The public restoration of the Society throughout the world in August, 1814, put an end to an embarrassing position, and Pius VII. paid no attention to the remonstrances of the Prince Regent and his Government, who desired to have no Jesuits in England.

The English Benedictine Congregation have had happily no such overwhelming events for their historian to record, as the Suppression and Restoration of the Jesuits. But they have had lately a provision for their future made by the Holy See, which marks the change that has taken place in England since the erection of the Congregation by Paul V. The present Pope has preserved for them their missionary character, a character to which England is so deeply indebted, both in ancient and recent times; and while they have been always monks, the Holy Father has promoted their monastic, without injury to their missionary, life. Two venerable titles have disappeared in these recent changes. The Benedictine Fathers on the mission were governed by two Provincials, styled respectively of Canterbury and of York. Their office has ceased to exist, and the government of the English Benedictine missions has been transferred to the Priors of the Monasteries to which the missioners belong. The monasteries have all along been subject to a President General, elected in General Chapter, and he continues to be the head of the English Benedictine Congregation. We may be allowed to express a hope that some of the monasteries may soon be raised to the rank of abbeys, with mitred abbots for their rulers.

The bond between the present English Congregation of the Order of St. Benedict and the ancient English Benedictines was Father Sigebert Buckley, the last survivor of the monks of Westminster Abbey, who had been professed by that Confessor of the Faith, Abbot John Feckenham. Dom Sigebert Buckley was ninety-three years old when he died, and he had spent forty-five years in prison for the Faith. In the Gatehouse prison he admitted two English Fathers to profession as monks of Westminster, on the 21st of November, 1607, and after them ten more. Others who had been professed in Spain were united into one Congregation with the English by Paul V. in 1619. Their first General Chapter was held in 1621 in St. Gregory's, Douay, a monastery which with those of St. Laurence at Dieulwart and St. Edmund's at Paris had been founded by the English monks from Spain. St. Benedict's monastery at St. Malo had also been founded from Dieulwart. This last house has now no representative, as it was transferred in 1699 to the Congregation of St. Maur; but St. Gregory's is now at Downside, St. Laurence's at Ampleforth, and St. Edmund's at Douay, which has lately sent a branch to Malvern.

We have seen that in 1773 the Vicars Apostolic reported to the Holy See that there were 44 Benedictines engaged in missionary work in England. There are now 105, together with 6 Fathers at the Cathedral Priory, Clehonger, 19 Fathers at Downside, and 15 at Ampleforth. The work of the College at Douay will not be interrupted in consequence of the transfer of St. Edmund's Priory to Malvern. There are now in England three Benedictine houses of other Congregations, Erdington of German monks, Buckfastleigh of French, and Ramsgate of the Congregation of Monte Cassino. The missionaries of the English Congregation are most numerous in the diocese of Liverpool, in which city they have four churches. They are, after this, strongest in the dioceses of Hexham and Newcastle, Birmingham, and Newport and Menevia. The ancient Western District had seven Benedictine Vicars Apostolic and three Franciscan. On the erection of the see of Menevia and Newport, it was given to the English Benedictines, together with its Cathedral Chapter, as a memorial of the position held in England by the Benedictine Order before the Reformation, when nine of the most important Cathedrals were theirs, and twenty-four of their Abbots had seats amongst the spiritual peers in the House of Lords.

The Congregation of English Franciscans, which was founded in 1617 by Father John Genings, the brother and biographer of the Venerable Edmund Genings, died out by degrees and is now gone. One of the last survivors was in turn first Bishop of Clifton and of Nottingham. There are now in England about 60 sons of St. Francis, including the Capuchins and the various Congregations of Franciscans.

The Order of St. Dominic has some important houses with, in all, about 40 Fathers in England. Their Novitiate is at Woodchester, and they have priories at Haverstock Hill, at Newcastle, at Leicester and at Hinckley, together with some other missions. Cardinal Howard in the seventeenth century founded the house of English Dominicans at Bornheim, which Woodchester now represents.

The Cistercians have our only English abbey, with a mitred Abbot, at Mount St. Bernard's in Leicestershire. It is an English house, of which we may well be proud. The Carthusians of the Grande Chartreuse have recently founded a Charterhouse on English soil. St. Hugh's at Parkminster enables us to realize what our old Carthusian cloisters and churches were like. Other ancient Orders are also reappearing amongst us. The Premonstratensians are in several places, of which the most remarkable is Farnborough Priory, erected by the Empress Eugenie as a resting-place for her husband and her son. We have also some Canons Regular of other Congregations, but as yet few in numbers, and besides two houses of Carmelites, a house or two of Servites, one of the few Religious Orders that did not exist in England before the Reformation.

There are Religious Congregations also to whom England in recent times is greatly indebted. Father Gentili, of the Fathers of Charity, was the first to preach public missions or retreats in England, and his work was accompanied with signal success. The Fathers of Charity are strong in England. Their Novitiate is at Wadhurst in Kent; they have long had a flourishing College at Ratcliffe near Leicester; they have acquired St. Etheldreda's Church in Ely Place, the chapel in ancient times of the London house of the Bishops of Ely; they have the Reformatory at Market Weighton; and they have missions at Rugby, Newport, Cardiff, and Loughborough.

The Passionists have about 40 Fathers engaged in the English mission, and they have also charge of an English church in Paris. Father Dominic, who died in the odour of sanctity, was a close follower of St. Paul of the Cross in his love for England. To this devoted Father was allotted in the Providence of God the happy lot of being the priest who was called upon to receive the late Cardinal Newman into the Church at Littlemore. Another Passionist Father to whom we owe much was Father Ignatius Spencer, who went about Europe preaching a crusade of prayers for the conversion of England. His example should never be forgotten, and his crusade of prayers should never cease. He was the first of the notable converts of the nineteenth century. He was the brother of the Earl Spencer of that generation, and renouncing his living of Great Brington in Northamptonshire, he became a Catholic. After his ordination, he was Dean at Oscott College; and afterwards becoming a Passionist, he laboured zealously till his death in 1865. This death was in accordance with his own desire, a lonely death by the roadside.

The Redemptorists devote themselves, almost exclusively, to the important work of missions and retreats. Their three houses in England are at Clapham, Bishop Eton, and Teignmouth, and their numbers are under 40. There are still several Congregations left unnamed, the Marists, the Oblates of Mary Immaculate, the Pious Society of the Missions, the Vincentians, and others who as priests, have care of souls; and several teaching Congregations, consisting of Brothers only.

To these must be added, as occupying an intermediate position between the Regular Orders and the Secular Clergy two Oratorian houses, each of which in its own way has left its mark upon our generation. The Birmingham Oratory was founded by Cardinal Newman, who was its Superior till his death eighteen months ago. He attached to it the Edgbaston School, where now are the sons of the first generation of its boys. The London Oratory for many years had Father Faber for its Superior, whose hymns, whose sermons and ascetical writings, and whose series of *Lives of the Saints* have leavened the minds of English Catholics.

Reckoning the Oratorians and the Oblates of St. Charles as Secular priests, the *Directory* of the present year gives us 841 Regulars and 1,701 Secular priests as the clergy of England and Wales, leaving out of account some communities of exiles, but including all those in monasteries and colleges. The proportion of Regulars to Seculars was beyond comparison larger in 1773, the Bishops' reports to Rome giving 217 Regulars to 175 Seculars. The very large increase in the numbers of the Secular Clergy within these last years is one of the best signs that the Church in England is steadily reverting to her normal position.

Before speaking of the religious houses of women with which the country is now studded, the multiplication of which is another sign of God's merciful regard, we must first give a glance at the Colleges to which we owe our increased supply of Secular priests. In this respect the old Secular College at Douay had done more for England than all the other Seminaries put together. It was the foundation of Dr. (afterwards Cardinal) Allen in 1568, and it saved England from the extinction of the Catholic religion by the loss of its clergy. The College was in a most flourishing condition, when it was overwhelmed by the French Revolution. When the College at St. Omers, which was founded in 1593 by Father Persons as a school for English lay-boys, was left by the Jesuits in 1762, the vacant building was handed over to the English Secular Clergy with the title of a Royal College. Its first president was the Hon. and Rev. Thomas Talbot, and when he became Coadjutor Bishop in the Midland District in 1766, Alban Butler succeeded him and died there in 1773. When the Revolution destroyed these two Colleges, the Rev. John Daniel was President of Douay, and the Rev. Gregory Stapleton of St. Omers. After many adventures and hardships and long imprisonment, the Superiors and Professors of the Secular and the Benedictine Colleges at Douay, and of the Secular College at St. Omers, together with the boys of their Colleges that had not succeeded in previously making their escape, received permission to leave France, and on the 2nd of March, 1795, they crossed over to England. Sir Edward Smythe hospitably gave up his house at Acton Burnell to the community of St. Gregory's, Douay, who removed to Downside in 1814.

Bishop James Talbot had bought Old Hall Green in Hertfordshire and opened it as a school for lay-boys in 1769. The school had previously been carried on for a time at Standon Lordship, Lord Aston's place, not far off, and before that, from 1696 to 1745, a similar school had existed at Twyford near Winchester. Twenty refugees from Douay had been conducted to Old Hall by Bishop Douglas, in 1793, on the feast of St. Edmund the Archbishop, which Saint was taken as the patron of the College. Dr. Gregory Stapleton, on his arrival from St. Omers, was made its President, and he had under him some of those who had escaped from St. Omers and Douay.

In the first instance some few Douay students who belonged to the Northern District remained at Old Hall, but these were summoned to the north by Bishop Gibson, who had begun a

College at Crook Hall, with the Reverend Thomas Eyre for President and Mr. John Lingard, not yet in orders, as Vice-President. The place of President was given to the Rev. John Daniel, the last President of Douay, but he resigned it after a few days to Mr. Eyre, in order that he might retain the title of President of Douay, so as to be in a position to claim compensation from the French Government for the property seized at Douay. In 1815, an indemnity was paid to the English Government, which was spent on the Pavilion at Brighton for the Prince of Wales. It is hard to see how our Government could justify its acceptance of money that belonged to its Catholic subjects, if it had conscientious scruples on giving the money to its owners. The College at Crook Hall, which in 1808 was transferred to Ushaw, was exclusively composed of refugees from Douay. It directly succeeds the old Secular College at Douay, and Old Hall succeeds to St. Omers, which itself was, in its secular state, a filiation from Douay.

St. Mary's College, Oscott, was founded by Bishop Milner as his Episcopal College in 1808. It had previously existed for twelve years under lay governors of Cisalpine sympathies, with the Rev. Dr. Bew as its President. The Rev. Thomas Potts was appointed by Bishop Milner, and continued, at least nominally, to be President till his death in 1819, but the Rev. John Quick performed his duties for nearly three years. The Rev. Thomas Walsh, who was consecrated Bishop in 1825 as Dr. Milner's Coadjutor and successor, and the Rev. Henry Weedall, afterwards Domestic Prelate of His Holiness, were the next Presidents; and then came one whose reputation gave the College a great name. Nicholas Wiseman, afterwards Cardinal and first Archbishop of Westminster, came to Oscott in 1840 as Coadjutor to Bishop Walsh, then Vicar Apostolic of the Midland District, and left it when he was made Pro-Vicar Apostolic of London in 1847. In Bishop Milner's time, the College began with about five-and-forty boys, of whom a few were intended for the priesthood. It was partly secular and partly ecclesiastical, as Old Hall was, and as Ushaw and Prior Park still are. Bishop Ullathorne opened a strictly ecclesiastical Seminary at Olton, following herein the example of Cardinal Manning, who had removed his Church boys for their higher studies from Old Hall to St. Thomas's Seminary at Hammersmith. The Seminary was removed from Olton to Oscott by the present Bishop of the Diocese, and Oscott now is an exclusively ecclesiastical Seminary. The Episcopal College for Liverpool is at Everton, and the Seminary at Upholland near Wigan.

In 1829, Bishop Baines, a Benedictine who was secularized by Pius VIII. when he succeeded Bishop Collingridge as Vicar Apostolic of the Western District, bought Prior Park near Bath. He intended the central house to be his episcopal residence, and he meant the two wings, called respectively St. Peter's and St. Paul's, one to be a Seminary, the other a College for lay-boys. The place was devastated by a fire in 1836, and becoming in consequence involved in difficulties, it was sold to Mr. Raphael, an Armenian Catholic, at whose death it was reacquired by the Bishop of Clifton, who has restored it to the uses for which Bishop Baines intended it.

It is unnecessary in this place to give any sketch of the history of all the Colleges now happily existing in England. Mention has already been made of the Oratorian School at Edgbaston, and of the College of the Fathers of Charity at Ratcliffe. The Society of Jesus has, besides Stonyhurst, Beaumont near Windsor, Mount St. Mary's near Chesterfield, and a day-college in Salisbury Street, Liverpool. It is hoped that before long another Jesuit day-college may spring up at Wimbledon in the diocese of Southwark.

The Anglo-Benedictines have Colleges at Ampleforth and Downside, and the Cassinese Congregation at Ramsgate. St. Wilfrid's College at Cotton near Cheadle is the new home of the ancient school of the Midland District that did such good service at Sedgley Park. St. Mary's College, Woolhampton, does similar good work in the south of England. The Oblates of St. Charles founded a College in London in 1863; the Society of the Sacred Heart for Foreign Missions has a College for missionaries at Mill Hill; St. Bede's College at Manchester is under the Bishop of Salford; St. George's College, Weybridge, is conducted by the Josephites; Tooting College by the Brothers of Christian Schools.

To our Colleges in England we must add those still existing as Seminaries for the English clergy on the Continent. The first of these is the venerable English College at Rome, the first founded after Douay to supply the English Mission. It began in 1579, and to it has been added by Pius IX. the Collegio Pio, named after him, and founded by him in 1852. There are also Valladolid and Lisbon, dating back the one to the sixteenth, the other to the seventeenth century. They are all of them now under the management of the secular clergy, but the two first named were conducted by the Jesuits up to the time of the suppression of the Society. These three Colleges prepare their students for the priesthood. The Benedictine College at Douay takes boys at an earlier stage in their studies, and sends them elsewhere for their philosophy and theology. These four English Colleges on the Continent continue to render great services to the mission in England, and they are held in affectionate regard by all their old students.

In speaking of the convents in England, we must be brief, far briefer than the interesting histories of many of them deserve. One single community that existed before the Reformation has come down to our time. The Bridgettine Nuns of Sion House, near Isleworth, went into exile on the accession of Elizabeth, and after much wandering in the Low Countries, settled down at Lisbon. Some years since they came to England, and are now at Chudleigh.

The first convent founded for English religious women after the Reformation, was the Benedictine Monastery of the Assumption founded at Brussels, in 1598, by Lady Mary Percy with Dorothy and Gertrude Arundell. In 1794, this was the first of our English convents to reach England, when driven from its old home by the French Revolution. After a long stay at Winchester, St. Mary's Abbey has been transferred to East Bergholt, near Colchester.

The first filiation from the abbey at Brussels was the Abbey of Our Blessed Lady of Comfort at Cambray, founded in 1623. It is now at Stanbrook, and it is the only Benedictine convent in England subject to the Regulars of the Order.

The convent at Ghent was founded from Brussels in 1624, and was called the Abbey of the Immaculate Conception. It is now St. Mary's Abbey at Oulton.

The Priory of Our Blessed Lady of Good Hope was a colony from Cambray, commenced at Paris in 1652. This community is now St. Benedict's Priory, Colwich, and it has had the devotion of the Perpetual Adoration of the Blessed Sacrament in constant practice since 1829. St. Scholastica's Priory at Atherstone was an offshoot from this monastery in 1858.

In 1652, Ghent sent a filiation to Boulogne, which was

transferred, in 1658, to Pontoise near Paris. In 1786, this community was dissolved, the Abbess and one half of the Sisters joining the Abbey of Dunkirk. This also was a filiation from Ghent, founded in 1662. In the French Revolution, the nuns were very hardly used, being imprisoned with other communities at Gravelines. When they reached England in May, 1795, the old convent at Hammersmith was given to them, and there they remained till 1863, when they removed to St. Scholastica's Abbey, Teignmouth.

The Revolution has also given us St. Mary's Priory, Princethorpe, a French house that came here from Montargis, and has remained here and become English.

These are all Benedictine Houses; but the Revolution sent over to us other English houses of various Orders. The Priory of Our Lady of Reparation at Carisbrooke was founded, in 1661, by Cardinal Howard at Vilvorde. They are Dominicanesses, subject to Regular Superiors. The Third Order of St. Dominic was introduced into England, under the late Archbishop Ullathorne, by Mother Margaret Hallahan, whose Life reads like that of a saint. Their chief houses are at Stone and at Stoke-upon-Trent. St. Clare's Abbey, Darlington, represents the house of Poor Clares founded at Gravelines in 1609, and its two filiations; that of Aire dating from 1629, and that of Rouen from 1648. Our Lady of Dolours at Taunton, of the Third Order of St. Francis, was first established at Brussels in 1621, and afterwards moved to Nieuport and Bruges. The Teresian Carmelites at Lanherne began at Antwerp in 1619, and the convent at Darlington came from Lierre, a colony in 1648, from Antwerp. The English Canonesses of the Holy Sepulchre, founded at Liège in 1616, are at New Hall. Those of St. Augustine at Abbotsleigh were at Louvain, having begun in 1609. The Louvain convent had sent a colony to Bruges in 1629, which is there still, the only convent that returned to the Continent when the revolutionary storm subsided. It has, however, lately sent a filiation to Hayward's Heath, and South Mimms is a colony from Abbotsleigh. The house of the same Order at Neuilly was founded in the Rue des Fossés St. Victor in 1633. This was the only English house on the Continent that did not take refuge in England during the French Revolution.

The Institute of Mary, which is still very flourishing in Bavaria and other countries under the title of the *Englischen Fraülein*, represents Mary Ward and her companions. There were two houses in England: one at Hammersmith, which died out, and St. Mary's Convent, York, which was founded in 1686, and is the most ancient religious house in England, remaining in the place of its original foundation. Houses dependent on Bavaria are at Ascot, and at Haverstock Hill, and some houses have been founded in England by the Irish branch of the Institute, better known as Loretto Nuns.

The first trace of any of the modern congregations of nuns is to be found in Bishop Griffiths' report to Propaganda in 1837, in which he says that besides two Benedictine Convents and that of the Holy Sepulchre, he had also two houses of the "Faithful Companions." Four years after this the "Good Shepherd" began its work in London. If we now add that there are from four hundred to four hundred and twenty houses of religious women in England at this moment, including small houses of the Sisters of Charity of St. Paul, who establish themselves in small communities of three or four nuns to teach parish schools, but including also a very large number of numerous and flourishing communities, belonging, in all, to about eighty independent Institutes, it will be clear that it is quite impossible to give even a few words to the history of their beginnings. It is a marvel of God's providence how they are supplied with subjects and how they are maintained. It may possibly be thought that convent schools for young ladies are too numerous; but it is impossible to admire too much the splendid religious spirit that exists in our convents, or the self-denying and hardworking lives that our nuns lead.

Besides those already mentioned, the Nuns of the Sacred Heart, of Notre Dame, and of the Holy Child, the last-named being of English origin, are the principal Institutes for teaching girls of the upper classes. Many middle schools and very many more schools for the poor are taught by nuns; while the schoolmistresses in secular schools have almost all of them been through a special training, under the care of nuns, at Mount Pleasant in Liverpool, and at Wandsworth. The Training College for schoolmasters at Brook Green owes its existence and maintenance to the zealous care of the Catholic Poor School Committee. Other charitable works, besides education, are in the zealous hands of Religious, for instance the nursing of the sick by several Institutes of Nuns, and the care of the aged by the Little Sisters of the Poor and the Poor Sisters of Nazareth.

It is not only for bringing colleges and convents to England from the countries that gave them hospitality in the days of persecution that we are indebted to the French Revolution. Another signal service was rendered to the Catholic religion in England by the expulsion from France of the flower of the French clergy and laity. Every one knows that we gave hospitality to the *emigré* priests, but very few are aware of the number of those that took refuge on English soil. At one time we had from eight to ten thousand French priests in the country, who came over between 1792 and 1799. There was a large voluntary subscription for their maintenance, and this proving inadequate, the Government added £7,830 a month for the support of the priests, and £1,000 a month for laymen. In the King's house at Winchester there were 700 priests collected together at one time, while 165 others were housed in the same town. Some of the latter were badly treated by the mob, which is hardly wonderful when it is remembered that they united in themselves the two characters that were most unpopular at that time in England. They were Frenchmen and priests. The real wonder is that on the whole they should have been so favourably received. Little unpleasantnesses there must have been. For instance, the Mayor, the Chancellor, and magistrates of Winchester petitioned that the Abbé Jacques Couvet might be sent away for proselytizing. It was but little that he had done or said, but he was removed to another place, and he died after some time at Carshalton. The French priests were in a very difficult position and they behaved with great prudence: the English were full of the strongest prejudices, but their humanity and generosity were still stronger. The University of Oxford, not venturing to print a Breviary for their use, gave them an edition of the Vulgate printed expressly for them. The exiled clergy were scattered about freely, in addition to the large number who lived together in community at Paddington, Reading, Tame, and elsewhere. The priests worked for their livelihood with the greatest diligence at a thousand incongruous occupations. Nothing that they could do was left untried, even to agricultural labour. Two hundred of those at Winchester worked at tapestry, provided for them by the Marchioness of Buckingham, who was secretly a Catholic. Some, though comparatively few, obtained employment as teachers of French or of music. Some, fewer still, found opportunity for the one congenial work of the priesthood. As late as 1814 Bishop

Milner reported that he had 40 French priests employed among his clergy, of whom one half were about to return to France. In London, leaving out of account the chapels that were opened simply to enable them to say Mass, many missions owe their existence to the apostolic zeal of French priests, who supported themselves mainly by teaching, and devoted their little earnings to establishing chapels. Thus we owe Chelsea to the Abbé Fraynous, Somerstown to the Abbé Carron, Hampstead to the Abbé Morel, Tottenham to the Abbé Cheverus, and so on, with several more in London and in other parts of the country. The French chapel in King Street survives under something like its old conditions to this day.

There can be little doubt that the first blow to English anti-Catholic prejudices came from the *emigré* French clergy. Their conduct was most edifying under very trying circumstances, and the admiration entertained for their fortitude and fidelity led practical English people to think more patiently of their religion. More certain still it is that a blessing came to the nation from the hospitality accorded to them. Not only was the sacrifice of propitiation offered by thousands of priests on English soil, but the generosity that provided for the support of a large number of aliens, with whose country we were at war, and who were themselves priests of a detested religion, has been abundantly repaid by Him whose priests they were.

One thing, however, was unsatisfactory on the part of some portion of the French clergy, but it was not of a character to disedify Protestants. Pope Pius VII., in consequence of the Concordat made with Napoleon in 1801, called on the French Bishops to resign their sees. A certain number refused, and, notwithstanding that refusal, the Pope of his supreme authority suppressed all the sees in France and created a new Hierarchy. Unhappily some bishops and priests opposed the Concordat and declared that the Pope had exceeded his powers in the creation of a new Hierarchy in France. These schismatics were known as the *Petite Eglise;* and as in England their chief defender was the Abbé Blanchard, they were often called Blanchardists. In 1810 a test was agreed upon by the four Vicars Apostolic, but Bishop Milner alone enforced it. This diversity of discipline on a point of great importance was one of the causes of the division that unhappily divided the English Bishops at that time. In this as in all other points, Bishop Milner had the support of the Irish Bishops against his

Episcopal brethren. It was not till 1818 that all French priests in the London district, who were by far the most numerous, were called on as a condition for their exercise of the priesthood to sign the test. That test was a very simple one, declaring that Pope Pius VII. was "not a heretic nor a schismatic, or the author or abettor of heresy or schism." It seems incredible that through compassion for men in exile, smarting under the destruction of the venerable Hierarchy that had ordained them, so necessary a measure should have been left in abeyance so long.

It was the more necessary that such ultra-Gallican theories should be stamped out, as we were not entirely free from the taint of Gallicanism in some amongst ourselves. The very name of the Cisalpine Club and the avowed purpose of its existence show that, in various shades and degrees, Gallican principles were not unknown in England. It was natural enough that men should have minimized their Catholic position and tenets when they were striving to make themselves acceptable to a Protestant Government and Legislature, with a view to obtaining Emancipation. We may well be grateful that things went no further. Those who granted political emancipation were wise enough not to exact many conditions or disclaimers, and the reactionary effort to make ourselves as like Protestants as possible, soon passed away. The providence of God has brought us through it all, and that spirit is absolutely dead and forgotten. Nowadays it is simply impossible that an excellent priest should publish a "Liturgy, or Book of Common Prayer and administration of Sacraments with other Rites and Ceremonies of the Church, for the use of all Christians in the United Kingdom;" yet such a book was published by a good priest in 1812, and it found its way to the *Index* of prohibited books.

Such, of course, was not the general feeling of English Catholics, but the shadow of the penal laws passed away very gradually, and the fear of reawakening persecution undoubtedly made them timid and cautious. Mrs. Lingard, mother of the historian, who died at Winchester in 1824, in her ninety-third year, "remembered when her family used to go in a cart at night to hear Mass, the priest in a round frock, to resemble a poor man." The Rev. Joseph Berington was the first priest who appeared in black, and Dr. Husenbeth says that he was blamed for exposing priests to danger of persecution. The language of the preceding century still prevailed. Squire Tyldesley in 1712 writes in his diary, "I prayed at Crow Hall; went with Mrs. to Bowers to prayers; went early in the morning to prayers at Henry Mawdesley's:" meaning that he went to hear Mass. So Dr. Husenbeth notes that the Catholics in Dr. Milner's time "never spoke of hearing Mass, but used the word *prayers* instead; which habit was retained by most of the old priests down to a very late period," and he refers to the *Directories*, where at such or such a chapel it is mentioned that "*Prayers* are said at ten o'clock."

In those traditional days it was unusual for a priest to say Mass every day. Benediction of the Blessed Sacrament was very rare. High Mass was almost unknown. It was accounted frequent Communion to go at the eight Indulgences. The Roman collar did not come into general use till it was prescribed at the first Provincial Synod in 1852. Dr. Milner had the only cope in his district, and his crozier, made like a fishing-rod with a crook at the end of it, served also to open gates as he rode. Chapels were very poor, with nothing but a holy water stoup at the door, a poor altar and picture, and a tabernacle without a lamp; and the chapels were in back streets and out of the way corners. Many undergraduates have passed through their three years at Oxford, without being aware that there was a Catholic chapel in St. Clement's, though they passed close to it frequently. The church at Moorfields, for which the Corporation of London gave the site in 1817, was one of the first to be seen in a prominent position. We emerged from obscurity gradually and slowly.

But there was substantial virtue and merit under this unassuming exterior. Catholics in those days had the sterling solid religion that had been tried in the fire. Their fasting would make most of us feel ashamed of ourselves. If they went to the sacraments only at the eight Indulgences, they prepared themselves with care and long beforehand. They thought nothing of going long distances to Mass. Mixed marriages were almost unknown, and the children of the family were carefully instructed in their religion. As a rule there was but little intimacy between them and their Protestant neighbours, though there was much personal good-will and friendliness on both sides.

Their number it is not very easy to estimate. A return to the House of Lords in 1780 gave the total number of Catholics in England and Wales as 69,376. This if true would have been a sad falling off from the 150,000 or 200,000 at which they were estimated a century before. But it seems an understatement, for Lancashire alone in 1819, according to a detailed statement taken mission by mission, had then 73,500. Bishop William Gibson in 1804 computed the Lancashire Catholics at 50,000. The Bishop adds that "within the last 13 or 14 years the increase of Catholics has been very great, in consequence of the abolition of the penal laws" in 1788 and 1791; "and the liberty given to Catholic priests to celebrate worship and preach. There are now in Manchester, which is the largest city in England after London, 10,000 Catholics, although 14 years ago there were scarcely 600. The same may be said of Liverpool." In 1814 Bishop Poynter reported to the Holy See that his District contained in all 68,776 Catholics, of whom 49,800 were in London. At this time the Midland District was said to have 15,000 Catholics, and the Western 5,500. The want of an estimate for the Northern District makes it doubtful what the Bishops looked on as the number of English Catholics about the year 1814, but speaking roughly it may be taken as about 160,000, with 390 priests. About the year 1837 the reports to Rome say that there were in the country 508 priests. Unfortunately the Midland District makes no return of its Catholic population about that time, but judging by the returns of the other three Districts, the total at that time may be taken as estimated by the Bishops at about 400,000. Bishop Griffiths reckoned the London District as containing 157,314, and Bishop Briggs returned the Northern District as having 180,000 Catholics. The Western District made an extremely careful return of all its missions, reckoning its total Catholic population at 24,580.

In 1840 Pope Gregory XVI. created eight Vicariates in England instead of four; but as this measure was followed in ten years by the establishment of the Hierarchy, there is no reason for dwelling on this change.

CHAPTER V.

OUR HOPES FOR THE FUTURE.

WE now come to our own time, and to the events that have made us what we are. In numbers we are probably about a million and a half in England and Wales. Father Werner, the painstaking author of *Orbis Terrarum Catholicus*, gives 1,359,831, as the sum of the estimated Catholic populations of our fifteen dioceses in the year 1888. Our priests in the *Directory* of 1892 are given as 2,573. The increase is startling on the figures previously given.

Three things in the main have contributed, each in its own way, to produce this change—the Oxford movement, the Irish immigration, and the restoration of the Hierarchy. A few words about each of them are necessary in this place, and then a survey of our present condition and of our hopes for the future, will complete our task.

The Oxford movement may well be appealed to, as one of the strongest possible signs of God's merciful providence in our regard. It would be difficult to find the parallel to it anywhere. What nation is there, that after abandoning the faith, has shown a tendency to return to it? England shows that tendency most markedly, and the consoling thought is that it is not the work of men. If it were the result of the work of a great preacher or some zealous missionary, if a St. Vincent Ferrer, or a St. Francis Xavier had caught the ear and the heart of Protestant England, then it might be expected that when he died he would find no successor, and the movement would stop. But men have submitted themselves to the Church who have been utterly uninfluenced by living Catholics. The Holy Ghost has begun the work in their hearts, and brought it to completion, and men have come to the deliberate conclusion that it was their duty to become Catholics, though they knew no priest and perhaps hardly numbered any Catholics among their friends and acquaintances,

The Oxford movement began as a defence of the Church of England against Rome. It has brought many members of the Church of England to Rome; and it is safe to prophesy that in the future it will bring very many more. The movement began with a love of historic Christianity and a respect for the Fathers of the Church which led to a belief in dogma, a trust in sacramental grace preserved for us by the Apostolic succession, and obedience to ecclesiastical authority—in one word, the Oxford movement rested on the Visibility of the Church of God. It was an immense change to what had gone before. When the High Church movement began in 1833, there were two classes in the Church of England. As a matter of history there had been High Churchmen, but there were none then. There were the Evangelicals, who held the Pope to be Antichrist; and there was the High and Dry party, who regarded the Catholic religion as an effete superstition. The approach to the Church made by the High Church movement was very great indeed. It was not made from any love to the Catholic Church, nor from any desire to be like her. Hatred of the Church was universal. Emancipation was not given because men were more favourable to the Catholic faith than before. It was given because they could not govern Ireland without giving it: it was given in England with a certain contemptuous compassion, because we were such a helpless handful. And no sympathy with Catholic doctrine or practice animated the beginnings of the Oxford movement. The Protestant tradition had taken full possession of England, and the Universities were its stronghold. That the movement had in it the elements of an approximation to the Church was visible, but it was defended as the only safeguard against Rome. If the Anglican Church was Catholic, the Roman Church was not, at all events in England. And there was no other bulwark. The Protestantism of the Evangelicals was Lutheranism, pure and simple, and that at any rate was not the religion of the Fathers. English people began to think that they must have a Catholicism of their own, and though the Reformation had done a world of harm, especially by the destruction of the monasteries, yet it had, they thought, done this good, that it had given to the Catholic Church in England an opportunity to throw off Roman corruptions with the usurpations of the Papacy, and to make her doctrine and her practice pure and primitive.

Such was the start of the Oxford movement. Its results,

as far as they went, were Catholic and Roman ; its principles, in many respects, were Anglican and in reality Protestant. It was Catholic to believe in authority, in a visible Church, in the definitions of General Councils, in the Fathers as guides and witnesses ; but it was Protestant and Anglican to assume that the visible Church was divided, that the infallible voice was hushed, that patristic tradition was to be judged on arbitrary grounds, above all, that the modern Church spread through the world was not to be regarded as the sole judge of all controversy, invested with all the power that Christ had bequeathed to His Church, and that she had possessed at any time. Instead of this many a hard word was said of Rome ; all the harder that it was said in self-defence. But as time went on, the real purport of High Church doctrines began to be felt. It is no light thing to believe in dogma. It means that we hold this doctrine, because it is God's revealed truth. It is true that High Churchmen sought for their dogmas on the Protestant principle of private judgment, applied to the Fathers and to antiquity, instead of to the Bible alone. But one dogma led to another, and the study of antiquity testified more than men expected to the primitive character of Catholic doctrines and practices. Regeneration in infant baptism was clearly patristic, and as clearly it was thought to be professed by the Church of England. It was not till 1851 that it was ruled by the Queen in Council to be an open doctrine in the Anglican Church, to be held or not held, taught or not taught, in her churches as her ministers chose. But the High Church doctrine of the regeneration of infants in baptism spoke volumes as to the efficacy of sacraments. Were then only two of Divine origin ? That was not the teaching of the Fathers. And then with respect to the greatest of the sacraments, the Blessed Eucharist, what was meant by the Real Presence ? John Keble, the poet of the movement, first wrote

In the heart,
Not in the hands, the great High Priest
Doth His own self impart.

And then in later editions of his *Christian Year,* he altered the words into "In the heart, as in the hands." How that could be except by Transubstantiation could not easily be seen. The Real Presence was due, not to the faith of the recipient, but to the Divine efficacy of the words of consecration. Such questions pressed on men's minds, and the result was that in 1841 Mr. Newman wrote Tract XC. to prove that the Thirty-nine Articles might be subscribed by men who held all Roman doctrine, and in 1844 Mr. Ward published his *Ideal of a Christian Church*, a Roman ideal and not Anglican.

The position was untenable, though strangely enough there were men so constituted as not to see it, and there are such men even now. Englishmen are practical by nature, rather than logical, but they are not impenetrable to logic. At least all of them are not. It is true that a multitude contented themselves with fallacies and inconsistencies, but it was not so with all. Does not a divinely constituted priesthood call for a divinely constituted sacrifice? Is there not more about the power of the Pope in Holy Scripture, than there is about infant baptism? Why should Episcopacy be accepted as of Divine origin, and the Papacy be rejected? How should the Church have had an infallible voice in four or more General Councils, and then have lost it? If the Church of God upon earth is but one, and that one Church is visible, how can that unity be any but a visible unity? How can there be a visible unity without a visible Head? Reason and common sense said that High Churchmen had gone too far to stay where they were. Consistency and logic must take them to Rome. They had prayed and preached against schism; were they to live and die in it?

In 1845 John Henry Newman was received into the Church. He was the real leader of the party, though by some strange freak the name of Dr. Pusey was given to it. Pusey remained behind. He was a learned man, but he had a very confused mind, and no doubt it is literally true to say that he did not see his way to follow Newman. Others remained who had followed Newman so far, but would not follow him to the logical consequences of his teaching. Some, in whom the force of prejudice was stronger than their reason, regarded it as an *argumentum ad absurdum*. The Catholic Church, they thought, must in any case be wrong, and if High Church doctrines led men to be Catholics, they must, for that simple reason and no other, be wrong too. Such men often became infidels, because they had not become Catholics. Others, like the late Dean Church, retained all they could of revelation, but thought consistency unattainable. A chivalrous affection for the religion they had professed and practised caused them to banish from their minds as unanswerable so simple an argument as that drawn from the unity of the visible Church. They worked hard and gave up thinking, and satisfied their consciences by forgetting the claim upon them made by a religion to which they were practically strangers. They continued where they were, by no means abandoning their High Church principles, and they have prevailed so far that, where infidelity has not won the day, the Church of England is leavened by sacerdotalism among the ranks of her clergy, to an extent that never has prevailed before. The laity are less affected by it than the clergy; but, speaking broadly, the religion now held by the Church of England is, with changes and modifications that do not alter its logical tendency, the continuation of that Oxford movement, the sole logical upshot of which was Rome.

But many came to the Church. That there should be conversions was not new. Bishop Douglas wrote from London to Rome in 1790: "The Catholic religion is now beginning to flourish, and as public services and sermons in the chapels are now permitted, many conversions are the result." In the same District Bishop Griffiths reported to the Holy See, in 1837, "Conversions are frequent. Last year 518 Protestants were converted to the Catholic faith in the London District. Of these conversions 390 occurred in London, and 128 out of London." Bishop Walsh, in 1838, said that, "in one part of his District," the Midlands, "and that not the most flourishing, he had confirmed 476 converts." In the year 1839 there were in the undivided Western District 221 conversions. In 1841 there were 101 conversions in Lancashire. In the scantiness of our statistics we may be thankful for such information, but we do not need it to assure us that conversions would take place as soon as the people could learn for themselves what the Church really was.

But the conversions that followed, and were the fruits of the Oxford movement, were different in quantity and quality from what had gone before. The accession of considerable numbers of persons of intelligence and education, especially clergymen, as well as many ladies and gentlemen of influence and position, the result of what, as far as we were concerned, was a spontaneous external movement, marked an epoch in our history and created hopes that time makes stronger. It is needless here to record the well-known names of the converts of note during the last half-century. It will be abundantly sufficient to notice that the *Catholic Directory* of the present year, in its list of Catholic Peers, gives the names of two Marquesses, seven Earls, and three Barons, who rank among Catholic Peers, through conversion to the faith. That is twelve peers out of thirty-nine, or forty, if Lord Morris' life peerage is included; and so out of fifty-four Catholic baronets the same may be said of fifteen, reckoning a convert who has succeeded to a baronetcy since the list in this year's *Directory* was compiled. These titles will not all continue, for want of Catholic heirs, but they serve to show how widespread was the movement. Its most striking feature, however, was the conversion of clergymen, many of them married men, who had to give up affluence, or at all events ease and comfort, for poverty and often severe privation. Every such sacrifice has brought its blessing to the land, and has helped forward the great work of its conversion.

Naturally such a movement, in spite of the conversions produced by it, as it claimed the prerogatives of the Catholic Church for the handiwork of Henry and Elizabeth, excited distrust on the part of Catholics. It is instructive to note it. Similar claims are still made, and Ritualists calmly assert their "continuity" with the ancient Catholic Church in England. We need not fear that the movement of the nation towards the Church will be checked by any such use of words. English people can hardly want to be told that a usurpation of titles does not bring with it the rights and powers of the ancient holders of those titles. A Protestant Archbishop of Canterbury is known to all the world to be something totally differing from a Catholic Archbishop of Canterbury, and the fact that the one desires to identify himself with the other in anything but the name, is a proof of the spirit with which Englishmen are learning to look back to the Church before the Reformation, and to desire to enjoy what their fathers threw away.

Whatever distrust Catholics in general may have had of the movement, there were some who instinctively felt what would be its result. One man in particular there was who followed that exterior movement sympathetically, and thoroughly understood its tendencies and its difficulties. Nicholas Wiseman, then Bishop of Melipotamus, residing at Oscott, wrote the paper comparing Puseyites and Donatists, that brought conviction to Mr. Newman's mind; and innumerable converts found a friend in him, both whilst he was Coadjutor Bishop at Oscott, and when he lived in London as Vicar Apostolic or Cardinal Archbishop of Westminster. A quarter of a century has passed since his death, and the Cardinal Archbishop of Westminster, who succeeded him, was himself a convert. Mr. Newman, after his conversion, was made by the Pope first a Doctor in Divinity, then Superior of the two Oratories of London and Birmingham, and lastly Cardinal. The converts, who have come, have found themselves at home in the Church. One of their number said that in the parable of the Prodigal Son, for them there was no envious elder brother. And if the reason be sought of this admirable harmony, it will be found in the perfect spirit of child-like submission with which the converts have yielded themselves up to their true mother. They have not come with theories of their own, nor have they thought of taking on themselves the *rôle* of reformers. They have happily been contented and delighted to find themselves ranked amongst the dutiful and loving children of the Church.

Another movement of a very different character has affected us almost as powerfully as the Oxford movement; but while the religious movement in the minds of men outside the Church touched the educated classes, this other became in a sense its complement, for it concerned the poorer classes only. There has been for many years a steady flow of Irish into England, and it has affected us English Catholics profoundly. It probably dates back to some extent to the Irish rising of 1798; it was largely increased by the Irish famine of 1845. The stream has stopped now, and while all along there has been more or less of emigration at the same time with the immigration, at the present moment and for some years past, many of the Irish have left and are leaving England. But still a great many remain, and they modify our condition and affect our position in various ways.

In the first place, the coming of the Irish has given us in many large towns a plentiful Catholic population. No Church could thrive without the poor to rest upon, and many of them. Without the Irish we should have had, comparatively speaking, no poor. It used to be said with truth that we had more than our proportion of well-to-do people. It is sometimes so said still, but now it is an entire mistake. What with the loss of many wealthy families, and the increased burdens and restricted revenues of many more, and what with the multitudes of Irish that the miseries of their own land have driven across the Channel, there is not a shadow of truth in it now. We have more than our proportion of those that need help, and far less than our proportion of those who can help them.

In Lancashire alone have we a large native Catholic population, and it is a very fortunate circumstance that the English and Irish Catholics in our Lancashire towns amalgamated perfectly. There are no race hatreds amongst them, or party spirit. They live happily and contentedly together, and when they intermarry, it is to the advantage of both races. Elsewhere, at least in towns, the Irish poor form the staple of our congregations. The priests may well be thankful that they have them to trust to, and certainly with their pence wonders have been done in many places. Priests feel greatly the loss of those who are leaving England for America and Australia, often the best of their flocks. And then, besides the direct good done by the fervour of many devout and holy souls amongst the Irish immigrants into England, and the blessing brought on our country by hardships and persecutions undergone by many in the practice of an unpopular religion in a strange land, very many promising boys of Irish origin have passed into the Seminaries of the English Bishops, and are now priests labouring with admirable zeal amongst the people, in perfect union and sympathy with the English priests on the same mission.

Alas, this is not all, for there is another side to the picture. We should be in a very different position now if only all our poor were what the best of them are. The Irish poor have so many admirable qualities that, if one evil had not prevailed amongst them, it is not too much to say that they would have converted all the English of their own class, amongst whom they have been thrown. They are in their normal state so full of faith, so attached to their priests, so large-handed out of their poverty, so hardworking, so frugal, as the harvesters used to show, so full of charity, and patience, and fervour, that if drink had not ruined many of them, they would have been the very salt of the land. In too many instances drink has despoiled them of their good qualities and made them neglect their religion. If their number in our prisons—for minor offences, it is true—is disproportionately large; if they continue to be hewers of wood and drawers of water; if their natural vivacity too often finds vent in quarrelsomeness instead of light-hearted merriment, it is drink that does it all. And if too many of them neglect their religion for years, if they get married by the parson or the registrar, if they marry without caring for the religion of the person they link themselves with, if they let their children be brought up anyhow, drink is the cause of it. Drink has undone numerous families of the most Catholic people upon earth, at least amongst those of them who have come to England.

There are, thank God, many everywhere to whom all this is inapplicable, and who have preserved their natural and supernatural good qualities untarnished in the midst of the seductions and temptations of our English cities. But almost every priest on the mission has to regret for many of his flock that they or their fathers ever came to England. That it should have been to them such a calamity is far from altogether their own fault. In their own country they were accustomed to be carefully looked after. If they were not at Mass, they were sure to hear of it. They lived under the eye of the priest, and in the midst of a strong Catholic public opinion. They have come to live in the slums of English towns, where the priest did not know them nor they the priest. There was no one to let the priest know where they were; and they were in what they knew was a Protestant country, ignorant perhaps that there was a priest within easy reach of them, and possibly disliking the thought of an English priest at all. Very likely, too, they were not the best who came over; and when they have come, the majority of those of whom we are speaking, lead so wandering a life that if a priest finds them out, he loses them again directly. They live crowded together in wretched rooms, and they are constantly moving in search of employment or because they cannot pay their rent. With everything squalid and miserable at home, it is hardly to be wondered at that the men should go to the public-houses for warmth, and brightness, and excitement, and company, or that if they go there, they should drink away their money, and leave their wives and children in want. The children swarming in the slums have had the other gutter children for playmates, and too often learn corruption before they come to the use of reason. What but a miracle could have prevented a frightful havoc among their souls, or have saved them and their offspring from being lost by the thousand?

There are two tremendous proofs of this most lamentable loss. One proof is that few priests in large town missions reckon as their Catholic population anything like that multiple of their baptisms that we learn from the Registrar General's returns to be the proportion between births and population. Every parochial census in our town missions, however carefully taken, falls too low. There must therefore be many Catholics in the parish who are not known to the priest. Thus the estimate of their population by the clergy of St. George's Cathedral in 1891 was 12,000; while their baptisms in the previous year were 626, which, multiplied by 25, would indicate 3,500 more Catholics in the mission. Peckham is estimated to have 3,300, but 170 baptisms speak of nearly a thousand more. Woolwich is said to have 3,200 Catholics, while its 246 baptisms seem to indicate over 6,000. On the other hand, Arundel, where three priests have charge of what they estimate as 1,000 Catholics, has but 34 baptisms or one to every 29 of the Catholic population. In Arundel, of course, the 300 Catholics or more, who are over and above the number indicated by the baptisms, must be converts, and many of the parents of the children baptized must be converts also. How could it be otherwise, if a thousand are now known to the priests by name, and when Canon Tierney died, some forty years ago, there were but 70 Catholics in the mission? But then, in the other missions we have mentioned, there are many converts, who ought to be added to the product of the baptisms, and thus the case is made still stronger. These missions have been taken as specimens almost at random, because by the Bishop's kindness the statistics are at hand; but many cases as strong or stronger could easily be found, if it were needful.

A second proof, even more forcible, is this. The statistics of all other particulars, except marriages, increase in a far greater ratio than the baptisms, and these again are utterly disproportionate to the number of Catholic marriages. Setting the marriages aside for a moment, let us look at the baptisms. There are many more children at school than there were, and many more adults making their Easter duties, yet the baptisms are about the same. If these, then, are a fair proportion for that number of baptisms—the Easter Communions cannot be in excess, and it is not in the case of these towns, but in country places rather, that Protestant children form a large proportion in our schools—what about the children who ought to have been at school, and the adults who ought to have made their Easter duties, year after year, for the five and twenty or thirty years last past? In the diocese of Westminster the baptisms in 1870 and in 1889 were about the same, but there are 7,177 more children at school, and 18,000 more Easter Communions at the later date than the former. Where were those seven thousand children in 1870, and where the 18,000 adults who ought then to have made their Easter? So too in the diocese of Liverpool, between 1875 and 1889 an increase in the baptisms of only 766, but an increase of children on the school rolls of 14,426, and Easter Communions increased by 35,093. Where were these thousands in 1875?

The consolation is immense to learn that things are better now, but that very improvement is itself an unanswerable demonstration of the miserable loss that has gone before. Let us take another instance and see how it tells. This time it shall be a single church, but a very important one. The expenditure on the Poor Schools of St. Chad's, Birmingham, the Cathedral parish, is now £1,500. Twenty-one years ago it was £350. Yet the children in the parish, owing to the opening of other churches, must be fewer now than then, for the baptisms in 1869 were 485, and in 1890 they were 357. It is true that the Government Grant in 1890 was £847 and in 1869 it was £292, but we are not discussing where the money comes from, nor blaming any one who had charge in 1869 or at any other time. The question remains, If £1,500 is needed now to teach the children of the parish, when the baptisms are less by a quarter than they were twenty-one years ago, what became of the more numerous children of that time when the total expenditure on their schools was £350? The lamentable fact remains, though there is no blame attributable to any one. At Birmingham, as in so many other large towns in England, the immigrant Irish poor came pouring in upon an over-taxed clergy, who did for them all that lay in their power, and who have gone on steadily working ever since, till they have brought themselves a little more nearly abreast of the needs of their people. All honour to those zealous priests for their persevering effort under grave difficulty, and eternal thanks to the goodness of God, who has rewarded their industry in behalf of all these souls. The appreciation they meet with elsewhere, is, to be told by the Archbishop of Canterbury that they have "effected a multiplication of edifices and institutions, but not of souls." Dr. Benson seems to think that our "edifices and institutions" have been erected for mere empty show. The truth is that they have been erected under the most pressing need, and our numbers have been multiplied by the acquisition of thousands of souls, who otherwise would have belonged, not certainly to the Anglican Establishment, but to the army of indifferentism and irreligion. The multiplication of churches and schools, and much more of priests, has led to the multiplication, not of nominal Catholics, but of children educated in their religion and of adults practising it.

For the education of our poor children as Catholics we are largely indebted to the Parliamentary Grant. If we had been left to our own money resources to build and maintain our Elementary Schools, we should have fallen hopelessly into the rear. The children would have been seized upon by educators of all sorts and utterly lost to us and to the Church. By an event as clearly providential as the coming over here of the *émigré* clergy and our own convents from the Continent in consequence of the French Revolution, our schools have been built and supported in considerable proportion by public money. When the Committee of the Privy Council on Education began to lay down rules for the distribution of the Parliamentary Grant, there was a strong unwillingness throughout the country to accept the Government help at the cost of Government inspection. The Catholic Bishops insisted on the appointment of a Catholic Inspector for the examination of our schools. This was conceded, and the arrangement lasted for many years, but now it has been swept away, and our schools are visited by Inspectors who are not Catholics and some of them even Protestant clergymen. As their examinations are limited to purely secular instruction, and the Bishops have for many years past appointed priests as Diocesan Inspectors to examine the children in their religious knowledge, no evil has resulted from the change. A trust deed was agreed upon by the Bishops for schools that were helped in the first instance by Building Grants from Government, and thus schools that were greatly needed in many localities have come into existence. The manner of the distribution of maintenance grants is no longer what it was in the beginning, but "payment by results" has been by no means an unfavourable criterion for us, and the latest change, involving gratuitous education to the poor, has undoubtedly also been favourable to us in the main. The Government very properly required a considerable portion of the cost of schools to be raised in the locality, and it is a marvel how this has been done through all these years, in spite of all the other heavy burdens of the missions. The effort to meet and deserve the Government Grant has been a great one, and it has been most successful. The schools throughout the country have been created during this period by the self-denying zeal of the clergy, and there is nothing to which we can turn with more satisfaction and hopefulness. We may be sure that an attempt will before long be made to deprive us of the Grant, and at all Parliamentary elections every Catholic ought to obtain a promise that the candidate for whom he votes will support the Voluntary Denominational Schools.

It is impossible to speak of our Elementary Schools without a word of gratitude to the Catholic Poor School Committee, which dates from before the Hierarchy. It was founded by the Bishops in 1847 to look to the interests of our Elementary Schools, and we are greatly indebted to it and to Mr. Allies, who for the greater part of its existence has been its active and able secretary. The Committee has been the mouthpiece of the Bishops in their negotiations with the Education Committee, and its management of our school affairs has justified the perfect confidence reposed in it by the Bishops. We mainly owe the establishment of our excellent Training Colleges, without which the multiplication and efficiency of our schools would have been impossible, to the Poor School Committee. One of its most satisfactory features has been the hearty co-operation of priests and laymen. Catholic gentlemen have freely given their time and labour in serving on the Poor School Committee, foremost amongst whom was the Hon. Charles Langdale, for many years its chairman. May they ever be ready to render the Church such service!

In 1850 Pope Pius IX. gave us our Hierarchy, and it was received with a storm of anger by Protestant England. There was something, perhaps, in the form of the Pastoral from "the Flaminian Gate" that Cardinal Wiseman would never have written, if he had foreseen the temper which it would arouse; but he made ample amends by his splendid "Appeal to the Common Sense of the People of England." The sole legislative effect of the violent outburst of anti-Catholic public feeling was a futile Act of Parliament which has since been repealed without once having been put into execution. The social effect was deeper. The upper classes did not suffer long, but Catholic servants and all in the working classes had very much to bear.

The outcry died out at last, and many who had joined in it have since looked back upon it with a sense of shame. It is unlikely that educated men will ever join in such a clamour again, not from their regard for us, but because unhappily infidelity and indifferentism have made sad progress. But a popular commotion against Catholics is still quite amongst the possibilities of our position, though the results of a violent outburst would in the long run be in our favour. The mob of our day is much the same as the mob that, in June 1852, burnt the chapel at Stockport, and kicked the tabernacle about the streets.

As far as the Catholic Church in England is concerned, the establishment of the Hierarchy has been an unmixed good. The demand for it was of very ancient date, but it could not well have been granted when the request was not made in a good spirit. The Catholic Committee in 1783 asked for it " that the frequent recurrence to Rome might cease." This was a piece of noxious ignorance, which was meant for England and not for Rome. In a very different spirit to this, Bishop Poynter in 1815 urged on the Holy See that the restoration of the Hierarchy was much needed. All the Vicars Apostolic petitioned for it in 1845, and two years later Bishops Wiseman and Sharples, and later still, Bishop Ullathorne, went to Rome to represent the wish of all the Bishops. Apostolic Letters were drawn up in 1847, by which the eight vicariates were erected into so many dioceses, but it was not before the 29th of September, 1850, that Pius IX. published his Brief erecting the archbishopric of Westminster with twelve suffragan sees. Two of these dioceses have since been divided, so that there are now fifteen sees in England, which constitutes the Ecclesiastical Province with the largest number of suffragan bishoprics at present existing in the world.

The Pope's intention had been to have made Bishop Wiseman a Cardinal, and to have required him to reside in Rome. Happily for England, Pope Pius IX. changed his mind and sent Cardinal Wiseman to us to be our first Archbishop of Westminster. No one can fail to see the hand of God in the appointment of our first and of our second Archbishop. Each one has been the man of his own time. The country that received Cardinal Wiseman with outrage and insult on his first arrival, learnt to value and respect him, and his funeral was a triumph. His successor had no such hostility to live down, but year by year he advanced in the appreciation and regard of Englishmen, and the feeling of multitudes about his funeral was but carrying out to the end what had been the popular regard for him during his life. This is not the occasion to attempt the sketch of what we English Catholics owe to these great men. Suffice it for us to think what we should have been without them, to raise in our hearts the gratitude due to God, who gave Milner and Challoner to our fathers and grandfathers, and who has provided for our more critical times still more providential men. The care that our Heavenly Father has taken of us in the past would have made us ashamed of ourselves if we had looked forward with misgiving to the future.

Westminster has now received from the hands of the Pope its third Archbishop. May his reign be long and prosperous! Salford shows us what Westminster as a diocese may expect at his hands, and the prospect fills us with hope. The Archbishop has a double field of work. He is not only our most dignified ecclesiastic, holding a most prominent position in the sight of the whole country, but he is also the pastor of a vast diocese, which stands in need of all a pastor's care. The new Archbishop is the disciple of his two great predecessors, and he has had nearly twenty years' experience of the episcopate over a numerous clergy and a people exceeding in number those that he is now called upon to govern. His name and his deeds speak for him, and if Salford mourns, Westminster, and indeed all England, rejoices.

Before the restoration of the Hierarchy, the cry for it was often raised by those who were anxious to see our missionaries placed in the canonical position of parish priests. The institution of parishes throughout the country we were not ripe for, but Cathedral Chapters now exist in every diocese with duties modified to suit our circumstances. To the Chapters the Holy See has confided the choice of three names to be presented for the appointment of a new Bishop, when the see falls vacant. The Canon Law prevails in all ecclesiastical matters, subject only to such modification as special decrees of the Holy See may have sanctioned; and a body of appropriate local law has arisen from the enactments of our Provincial and Diocesan Synods.

Lately, and especially on the occasion of the Jubilee of the late Cardinal Archbishop, copious statistics have been published which show the large increase in the numbers of our clergy, of our churches, of the children in our schools, and of Easter Communions. The two most striking points respecting the diocese of Westminster, are that in the last twenty-five years the children in the elementary schools have doubled, and the Easter Communions increased by more than a thousand each year, the baptisms remaining much the same.

The table of these baptisms in the Westminster diocese may well be reprinted here.

	In 1850.	1865.	1870.	1870-4.	1875-80.	1889.
Infant Baptisms	5,719	7,975	7,197	7,080	6,891	7,208
Conditional Baptisms	581	1,164	1,190	958	1,135	1,300
	6,300	9,139	8,387	8,038	8,026	8,508

The fall and the recovery both of the number of infant baptisms and of conversions is very remarkable. The fall in the number of conversions was less, and the rally began sooner than that of the baptisms.

It is necessary to say that the number of priests in England and Wales when the Hierarchy was created in 1850 was 813. When Cardinal Wiseman died in 1865 it had risen to 1,338. It has now become 2,573. The other statistics recently published we may pass over, in order to find room for some that have not been collected before. They are of necessity partial, but they are valuable as specimens; and they may serve for comparison with the general statistics with which we shall be furnished when the results of the census are published.

In the diocese of Southwark the average of infant baptisms for the four years 1883–6 was 4,112, and for the next four years, 1887–90, it was 3,843, and of conversions for the last-named period 705. The estimate of the Catholic population of the diocese varies so much that it cannot have much value. That for 1891 was 86,925. The average Easter Communions reported for the three years 1884–6 was 28,744, and 32,998 for the four years following. The number given for 1891 is 37,519. The Catholic marriages for six years 1885–9 average 346, and the mixed marriages for the same period 175.

The clergy of Southwark are given in the *Directory* as 168 Secular priests and 139 Regulars; but these last include the French exiles who are not included in the total elsewhere, at least not in the diocese of Portsmouth. The great difficulty in the way of using the statistics of the *Directory* lies in differences of the manner of compilation. The number given above, 2,573, of the priests in England has this drawback, but the overstatement is very inconsiderable.

In 1884, Bishop Ullathorne made his last report to the Holy See on the state of the diocese of Birmingham; and this, to which we have been permitted access, we may compare with the Diocesan Inspector's report and the *Catholic Directory* seven years later. The baptisms in 1883 were 3,616, and in 1890, 3,461. The Catholic population of the diocese, as estimated by the clergy, was in 1883, 76,449; in 1890, 75,294. In 1883, in 158 schools there were 21,111 children; in 1890, in 164 schools there were 21,436 children. The priests in 1883 were 196, of whom 58 were Regulars and 138 Seculars; in 1890, there were in all 206 priests, 55 being Regulars and 151 Seculars. In the three years, 1881-3, there were confirmed 8,166, or on an average 2,722 annually; in 1890, the number was 2,596. The converts in the diocese for the same three years are reported by Bishop Ullathorne as 1,879, who adds that the perverts were 139; in the last three years, 1888-90, the conversions were as nearly as possible the same, that is 1,881, or for the diocese more than 600 converts each year.

In the diocese of Hexham and Newcastle the Catholic population was estimated in 1850 at 70,000, and the priests were 67; in 1875 at 121,000, and the priests 130. The priests are now 168. The baptisms have fallen from 6,469 in 1875 to 6,159 in 1889.

For the diocese of Newport and Menevia we can separate the counties and carry our comparison further back.

	Priests.		Baptisms.		Population.	
	1840.	1890.	1840.	1890.	1840.	1890.
Monmouthshire.........	7	19 ...	240	541 ...	3,264	10,525
Herefordshire	2	15 ...	50	42 ...	400	1,400
South Wales	4	41 ...	183	1,394 ...	2,305	30,604
Total	13	75	473	1,977	5,969	42,529

In all the cases given above the estimates of Catholic population are those returned by the clergy, and they are not made up by multiplying the baptisms. It is remarkable that in the table just given for Newport and Menevia, the baptisms for 1840 multiplied by 13 would give more than the number of Catholics as estimated, while now the multiplier is 21½. In other words, the priests know their people better now than they did in 1840.

The change in Lancashire in a long course of years is very noteworthy. Taking the county by its present ecclesiastical divisions, it had

	1819.		1890.	
	Priests.	People.	Priests.	People.
Salford	15	20,380	245	219,494
Liverpool	62	53,120	421	319,898
Total	77	73,500	666	539,392

In 1841, there were 119 priests, baptisms 9,375, Easter communicants 53,841, and conversions 649.

In contrast with the large numbers of these two great dioceses in Lancashire, let us take the diocese that contains the greatest number of square miles and the smallest number of Catholics of any in England. In the diocese of Northampton in 1890 there were 57 priests, in charge of 9,526 Catholics by their own estimate; the infant baptisms were 374, converts 233; 1,836 men and boys, 3,130 women and girls made their Easter duties, or 4,966 in all; the average attendance at Mass was 5,459; Catholic children of school age 2,312, on school rolls 1,795; average attendance of children at school, Catholics and Protestants, 2,929; marriages in the Catholic Church 55, of which 16 were mixed, and there were 6 mixed marriages contracted elsewhere. The total estimated Catholic population is 25½ times the infant baptisms. Now here there are 57 priests to take care of a body of Catholics that all together would form but a single parish in many of our large towns. The amount of converts, which is unusually large in proportion, is evidently due to the spade husbandry, so to speak, possible when the clergy have on an average less than 200 souls apiece. There are not likely to be many Catholics here who are not known to the priests.

One subject more there is deserving of some examination here, and it is the very anxious one of Catholic marriages, both mixed marriages and also marriages both parties of which are Catholics. Our marriages contracted in the Catholic church are lamentably few. This is shown by the Registrar General's returns, and much stress has been laid upon it by Mr. Gladstone,

In explanation of this low proportion, the poverty of the Irish in our great towns must be given as a very leading cause. They do not marry because they cannot afford to do so. A priest who has given this matter great attention writes: "The number of Irish unmarried men is notorious—not young men only, but middle-aged men and old men. The lodging-house is the resort of the unmarried man, and the lodging-houses are crowded with Irish. I do not speak of comers and goers, but of men who have been settled in the country for ten, twenty, and thirty years. Some intend to go to America and settle down there; others, and they are the majority, say that their wages are so low that they are hardly able to keep themselves, and they never think of getting married. There are ten unmarried Irishmen for one similarly situated Englishman. In Ireland in 1889 the proportion of persons married *per* 1,000 of the population was 9·1, whilst in England it was 14·7. In Ireland the birth-rate was 22·8, and in England 30·5. Of course the lower birth-rate follows the lower marriage-rate, but not in equal proportions."

To this must be added the very ugly fact that in large towns many Catholic marriages are contracted in the Protestant church. The same informant says on this subject: "Some priests think that this is done to avoid having to go to confession. This of course may influence some, but the chief cause is the bother of going to the Registrar, and the ease of turning in at the Protestant clerk's office and putting up the banns. I am certain that our marriages would increase 25 per cent. if we were rid of the Registrar. In the Protestant Cathedral at Liverpool and the Protestant Church of St. Nicholas there are some days three marriages, both parties of which are Catholics. I know a priest who takes a Protestant parochial magazine, which inserts all the marriages celebrated during the month, that he may find out those of his own congregation (often both man and woman) who have been married by the parson. I have reason to believe that this scandal is very rife in the large towns in Yorkshire and in the Midlands."

Besides the greater facility and the fact that no questions are asked, in many cases they are married much more cheaply at the Protestant church. The Registrar's fee comes to seven shillings, without including a certificate, and a Catholic marriage cannot be celebrated without the Registrar, according to the present law. In Catholic marriages the priest has often to forego his fee, because the Registrar has to be paid. This is hard, but the gravest hardship lies in the temptation to the poor to be married in the Protestant church, owing to the greater cheapness and facility.

It must be acknowledged with shame that such a practice shows that there are multitudes of the Catholic poor in our great towns on whom their religion sits very lightly. It is too true; but the fact can only be adduced to show neglect of the practice of their religion, which neglect is already shown by their absence from Mass and from their Easter duties. But still they are Catholics. By the term we understand those who have their children baptized in the Catholic church, and send for the priest when they are ill. Now the Registrar General makes his computation of the number of Catholics from the returns of Catholic marriages. Indeed he has no other data, but the considerations on which we have been dwelling show how it happens that his calculations are largely beneath the mark.

So far we have been discussing those marriages only in which both parties are Catholics, but when we turn to mixed marriages, it is yet more sad to find that in the majority of cases—still speaking of large towns and not of the country missions—these mixed marriages take place in the Protestant church without a dispensation from the Bishop, and consequently without any promise to observe the usual conditions. Here too, if it were not for the expense and trouble of the Registrar, many more mixed marriages would be celebrated in the Catholic church.

The priest, who has been already quoted, the Reverend Austin Powell, gives as his experience in his own mission of Birchley, in Lancashire, that, of 208 families, 85 are mixed marriages, and besides, there are 30 widowers and widows not now keeping house, who have had Protestant wives or husbands. Of these 115 mixed marriages, 7 were contracted in the Protestant church to 4 in the Catholic; the Protestant party has become Catholic seven times more frequently than the reverse; and of the children about a fourth are lost to the Church.

He then writes: "I am sorry to say that this is not a fair sample. Although in about five agricultural missions some little distance hence, the results are more favourable, in this, a mining district, my neighbours have suffered more severely than I have. There is not a congregation hereabouts where the mixed marriages are not in excess of purely Catholic marriages. In a church near to me, some ten or fifteen years ago, there was not a marriage during a period of three years celebrated by the priest, and yet the nominal Catholic population was 1,900." The Registrar General would not have recognized one single Catholic in the place.

Another example may be given, and this time it shall be a much larger parish. The Catholic population of St. Francis Xavier's, Liverpool, is estimated by parish census as 10,416. There are 2,230 families, and in 504 of these either the father or mother is not a Catholic. Of these mixed marriages 47 were contracted in the Catholic church, and 457 elsewhere. In 84 cases the Protestant party has become Catholic, and in 12 the Catholic has apostatized. Of the children 928 are being brought up Catholics and 193 as Protestants. In 43 families the children are being brought up Protestants, and in eleven some are Protestants and some Catholics. This means that, including 12 apostates, 54 Catholic parents have given up the religion of their children, either in whole or in part.

These figures are very instructive. Not a single Catholic would have been reckoned by the Registrar General for those 457 marriages: yet, discounting largely all the marriages in the Catholic church, there are 445 Catholic fathers or mothers remaining after 12 apostacies, converts say 37, and children say 890; in all 1,372 Catholics in a single parish, at the very least, who are known to the priests and are treated by them as part of their flock. It is probable that all these children are being brought up in the Catholic schools. The other statistics of St. Francis Xavier's may find place here. Of the 10,416 souls, 4,441 made their Easter duties in 1890, 7,400 have made their first confession, 6,759 their first Communion, 4,850 have been confirmed. Children of school age, 2,148; on the school books 1,805; examined 1,700; average attendance 1,474.

To this account of a large parish it may be interesting to add that of a country town. Skipton has 470 communicants out of 715 Catholics. Of these 202 may be called old English, and 81 converts and their children, making 283 English born. Born in Ireland 52, Irish born in England 213, those of Irish blood 163, in all 428 Irish, Germans 4; making a total of 715, of whom 457 were born in the place. In the 154 families 52 are mixed marriages, 38 in which the husband is Protestant, and

14 the wife. The children of these mixed marriages are 138, of whom 38 are apparently lost, and in 24 cases of the 52 mixed marriages 17 women and 7 men neglect to come to Mass. In 13 cases of mixed marriage the Protestant party has been converted, and in 2 cases the Catholic party has become Protestant. Of the 52 mixed marriages, 3 were in the Registrar's office, 3 in the Protestant church, 2 in Nonconformist chapels, and 44 in the Catholic church.

Another instance that may be taken is one of the districts into which the mission of St. Chad's, Birmingham, has been divided. Bishop Ullathorne selected it to put before the Holy See. The whole mission of St. Chad's the Bishop estimated at 7,125 souls, of whom 6,000 were poor Irish, a third of them moving every year. "Of 2,000 in one of the districts attached to the Cathedral, a careful inquiry showed that 456 never enter the church. In the district there were 98 mixed marriages, of which 25 were celebrated in the Catholic church, almost always the woman Catholic: keeping steady to her religious duties in 16 cases; in 73 neglecting religion and the education of the children; in 57 Mass not heard and Easter duties neglected for years; in 12 cases the promises broken; in 9 cases the children sent to Protestant schools; in 2 cases the Protestant party converted when sick."

It is needless to say that localities vary greatly. The cases that have been given are enough to show it. Indeed it is said that "conversions vary, not only in neighbouring missions, but even in different parts of the same mission." So do the mixed marriages, and so do the consequences of such marriages. But there can be no doubt that the effects are terrible. In two of the cases given one-fourth of the children of mixed marriages are lost; in St. Francis Xavier's a sixth; and at St. Chad's apparently 73 out of 98, or three-fourths. But there is much more evil that figures cannot show, for how can the induced indifference be numerically expressed, or who shall tell us what proportion of the children of mixed marriages persevere, even though they be sent to the Catholic schools? What happens in the next generation?

It has been said above that few priests will acknowledge their flock to consist of the number that their infant baptisms would indicate. It is of course misleading to apply one multiplier everywhere. The higher the birth-rate, the lower should the multiplier be; and as the birth-rate falls, the multiplier should rise. We have already seen reason to believe that the marriages of the Irish poor in England, including mixed marriages, are fewer in proportion to their numbers than those of the English around them. The question now arises whether, when they marry, they have larger families than the English. It is commonly thought that they have. The well-informed priest, from whom several quotations have been made, says: "I am convinced that the fallacy of the Irish being more prolific arises from the fact that they live in small houses, often several families in a house, the houses frequently packed in long courts, whence the children swarm into the main streets for a breath of air and for a sight of life, and hence passers-by are astounded at the number of children, not knowing how many families are closely huddled together, to which these children belong."

One other point has lately been mentioned, and it deserves consideration. The mortality amongst our Irish poor in their childhood is greater than that of the English about them. It is not to be wondered at. The moving from place to place, the herding together in filthy slums, the bad and insufficient food, all the consequences of their poverty, poor things, intensified by drunkenness, are more than enough to account for a disproportionate mortality.

As to the multiplier that should be used in order to deduce the total Catholic population from the baptisms, the mortality amongst the children is a reason for diminishing it, the fewness of the marriages and the consequent lowness of our birth-rate are reasons for increasing it, as well as, of course, the additions made to our numbers by conversions. We shall probably not be far wrong if we take that which belongs to the general population of the place. Speaking roughly this will be in populous places about 25 times the births.

This brings us within sight of the conclusion of our task. What is our present condition? What are our prospects? To what must we attend in the future?

And first for our present position. The worst is over. When the Irish came amongst us we had neither priests enough, nor churches enough, nor schools enough for them. We have lost thousands, not in workhouse schools only, but still more in the slums of our cities. There must be thousands in England with Irish blood in their veins, and indeed baptized by Catholic priests, who are now profoundly indifferent to all religion and absolutely ignorant of the Catholic faith. We are not yet provided with priests enough, or churches enough, or schools enough, but the worst is over, and the deficiency is not as appalling as it was.

Things are not as bad as they were when the Commercial Road mission had 1,030 baptisms a year, and only five priests. Yet things are far from right while Bermondsey had 457 baptisms in 1889, and 420 in 1890, and has but four priests. The Easter Communions in the last-named mission in 1890 were the number of the year, 1,890. Taking in those who have made their Easter at Melior Street, which is just out of the parish, and nearer to some of them, we may count the Easters as 2,000. And this out of at least 11,000 souls. There are more, far more, neglecting their Easter than those who make it, and this is looking only to those who take their children to that church to be baptized. There are 1,400 children on the books of 8 parish schools. The number is large, but there should be at least 2,000 children there. This is leaving to their own devices the thousands who have drifted away from their religion in the past fifty years, whose children and grandchildren are now in the Board Schools.

The Bishop of Southwark has lately cut Walworth off from St. George's mission. He has built there commodious schools, one of which serves as a good working chapel in the midst of the people, and he has stationed there two priests. The School Inspector of the Diocese reports an increase of children in the South London Schools of 1,147 as against last year. "The increase in South London is largely accounted for by the opening of the new schools at Walworth, which at the time of inspection, had on the school rolls 537 children. About a hundred of these, it is estimated, had been attending Catholic schools in the neighbourhood, but the bulk of them were drawn from Board and other schools." In other words, 437 Catholic children have been sent by their parents to a Catholic school now that one has been planted in their midst, which children would hardly have grown up Catholics but for this change. And as for the hundred who used to go to Catholic schools in the neighbourhood, their place has soon been filled, for the Inspector also says that "the schools connected with the Cathedral district show an increase of 156; those at Melior Street of 134; and those at West Battersea of 152."

Surely we have here the answer as to what is to be done. Perhaps the last thing done by Cardinal Manning for the good of his people was to assign a district, cut off from Bow and Poplar, in Bow Common to the Reverend Gordon Thompson. It was supposed to have taken 500 Catholics from one mission and 300 from the other. How many it will be found to have, is yet to be seen. The new mission starts in the midst of a dense slum in the East of London. Let any one who does not know what that means, go and see. This is what is wanted—God give us more of it! As a proof of the need, a friend says that "on Passion Sunday afternoon 150 children assembled, representing only a fraction of the full number who will have to be gathered together, but they were quite sufficient for a beginning. They were of all ages between three and fourteen or fifteen, most of them in tatters and terribly unkempt. Some had never been to school, some had been to Board or Wesleyan schools. To my great surprise, they fell at once into excellent order, and were as docile and tractable as could be desired. Moreover they learnt the unknown sign of the Cross, the Catholic version of the *Our Father*, and the *Hail Mary* with refreshing rapidity; so that it was quite possible to finish the lesson by saying a decade of the Rosary, for which many of them seemed to have much difficulty in finding their way to their knees. When I had had my innings, Father Gordon Thompson gave them a short catechism, and taught them a verse of a Catholic hymn with the harmonium, which was much to their liking. And then, with a distribution of brightly-coloured pictures, the school and the excellent order came to an end for the day. Many of these children seem to me almost painfully bright and intelligent in the midst of their destitution. There are some nice girls among them, in a 'raw material' state, and some splendid boys. Happily there is only one more Sunday to be tided over before the arrival of the nuns with their lay-helpers, when the work will be done in more orthodox fashion." It is enough to bring the tears to one's eyes to hear that these poor children serenaded the priest on St. Patrick's day, and knowing nothing else, sang for him some Protestant hymns.

In 1857 a large church was built in the Commercial Road district, one of the finest churches in London. The condition on which it was built was a promise that the mission should not be divided for a term of years. When that term came to an end, the Oblates of Mary Immaculate received charge of the Tower Hill mission, which was detached from Commercial Road. This was in 1866; Mile End had a slice of the Commercial Road mission in 1868; Wapping was taken out of it in 1872; and Limehouse had its share in 1880. Thus three-fifths of the old congregation of SS. Mary and Michael's, and more than three-fifths of the territory, have been cut off to form these four missions, either wholly or in part. Some further diminution is due to the fact that the people have followed the shipping to the Victoria and Albert Docks. Yet the infant baptisms still even now, after all diminutions, average 400 a year, which indicates 10,000 Catholics in the charge of four priests. The Catholic population in the East of London must have largely increased, for in 1860 there were in it but four missions with about 15 priests, and now there are 13 missions with 35 priests, and more if we count all the Regulars at Spicer Street, Tower Hill, and Forest Gate.

To return to SS. Mary and Michael's in the Commercial Road, at that time there were 25,750[1] Catholics with five priests and one church—a fine large spacious church, no doubt, where as many as 3,500 heard Mass on Sundays; but one church for 25,000 people,—five priests for 25,000 people! What could be done for the poor souls but teach the children who came to school, attend the sick-calls, hear the confessions of those who came to church, marry them if they asked to be married by the priest, carry on the services of the Church, each priest saying two Masses on Sunday and preaching frequently? Who shall say how many neglected to hear Mass, and to make their Easter duties? We may estimate them at about 20,000; and there would have been more if we did not allow for some who will have made their Easter in the neighbouring churches of Moorfields and Spicer Street. A mission preached in Lent would make a great difference, and in one year the confessions of as many as 7,000 different persons were heard between Ash Wednesday and Low Sunday. At the close of a mission preached by the Redemptorist Fathers in November, 1866, about 500 adults were confirmed. The work of the priests was as much as they could possibly do, without leaving them time or physical strength to visit the people in their houses,

---

[1] The Rev. Joseph F. Padbury, who was one of the clergy at Commercial Road at that time, writes that the total number of baptisms for the five years 1861-5 was 5,150, giving an average of 1,030 a year; and that the marriages for the same time were 750, or annually 150.

which is an absolute necessity of the highest order, if the poor Catholics are to be kept up to practice of their religion.

Far be it from us to blame the builders of fine churches. The splendid church built by Mrs. Lyne Stephens at Cambridge, and the stately successor of the dear old chapel in Spanish Place, are very, very welcome. It was time that we should come out of the catacombs; it was time that we should have churches and altars, of which we should not be ashamed; but building fine churches is not the way to provide for the Irish poor when they are clustered in thousands. They do not care for fine churches. They will not go far, and if the priest, and his church or chapel too, does not come to them, they drift away and are lost in the crowd. Two priests at Walworth with 2,000 people—it is a manageable number; and with 537 children in their schools, and their people all round them, within easy reach, we may hope that the evils we have spoken of may gradually disappear.

If an example be asked for in which the most excellent results of the policy of subdivision may be seen, the town to point out is Bradford, where Canon Motler has built church after church, going always himself to take charge of the colony he has last established. His new churches are, it is true, finer buildings than under such circumstances could have been looked for in the South of England; but he might well find imitators in many large towns in the spirit that has made him, like the queen-bee with the first swarm, lead the colony that he himself has prepared to go forth from the parent stock. Years ago, before the railways depopulated the Moorfields district, its Rector said that it took the mother church but six months to recover all the effects of a new mission being cut off from its territory. In six months' time the places of those who used to come to the mother church to Mass were all filled by others, and the money they used to give in the collections fully made up by new-comers. Meanwhile, a new mission had been started and a new centre established, baptizing its own children, conducting its own schools, collecting its own Easter communicants, and enabling many more to hear their Mass of obligation on Sunday, and to get to Confession and Communion at their convenience. It would be interesting to learn what difference to the churches at Bow and Poplar the opening of the new mission in Bow Common Lane has made. Is it too much to expect that in no long period of time, the zealous priest of the new mission may find himself in charge of 2,000 Catholics, instead of the 800 who have hitherto been a mile or three quarters of a mile from their chapels and priests, and that he will have 500 children gathered in his schools who have hitherto been in no Catholic school at all?

St. Chad's, Birmingham, has seen eight new churches spring up around it in thirty-seven years. Cardinal Manning, who estimated the number of the Catholics of his diocese at 180,000, wrote in 1890 that during his Episcopate "thirty-three new missions and seventeen stations, making in all fifty new centres, have been founded," and to this multiplication of centres, not to an increase of population, he attributed the increased numbers of the children and of Easter communicants. Our hope for the future is based on the increase of missions in large towns, so that the people may all be brought under the personal influence of the priesthood; and this we cannot regard as accomplished, until what we may call the normal state is attained, when every thousand Catholics are in charge of a priest within easy reach of them. No mission should be regarded as fully manned, till there is a priest for every forty baptisms.

This is what the poor want in our towns. Of the vast middle class, the backbone of England, what have we to say? Alas! only this, that it is the seat of all the bigotry in the country—that middle class, which is fast becoming the seat of political power. How are we to get at them, how secure a hearing, how appeal to their common sense? Our priests are rapidly increasing in numbers, and soon they will not be entirely occupied with the pressing work of saving our own. The day cannot be far off when they will be able to devote time and energy to the great work of the conversion of England. When the time comes, then those who so devote themselves will find the gain that it has been to have the name of Cardinal Manning become a household word in our middle classes, as that of Cardinal Newman has always been in the upper and educated classes of England.

At the same time, more must be done for the young men of the working class. Our elementary schools are filled with Catholic boys; but what becomes of them when they leave school? If they could but be somewhat better off in the things of this world: if they could but afford to marry Catholic wives, and settle down in the country, forming Catholic households, free from the curse of drink, and taking the place to which their intelligence entitles them, the future of our congregations would be assured. Can no one help them? More priests, living in their very midst, not jaded and worn out by the inevitable routine, but with time and energies to spare, to make friends of these young men, to spend their evenings with them, to know them personally and to take interest in them—this we may look forward to in the not far distant future, if God continues to multiply our clergy, as He has done since He gave us the Hierarchy. And not priests only, but laymen also, good, self-denying devoted laymen, mixing freely with those beneath them in social station, doing for them what is done for example at Newman House in Southwark, entertaining them, instructing them, showing sympathy with them, loving them.

To the upper classes we have the easiest access, and there more than elsewhere our work is done for us by those who know not what they are doing. Ritualism probably furnishes fewer converts than Tractarianism, because Ritualists are less Catholic in principle than the old Tractarians were. They have not the respect for authority that Newman taught his Anglican disciples. But then the Church of England would not tolerate Tractarianism, and it has been all but completely leavened by Ritualism. Ritualists have accustomed the country to the look of our priests and of our nuns, of our altars and our vestments and our ceremonies, and they preach our doctrines. Their disregard of authority has enabled them to do what the old Tractarians would have been driven out of the Church of England for doing. But the result is that the vast mass of Anglicans entertain very different feelings respecting our faith and practice from any that a short time ago could possibly have been anticipated. Let them go a little further, and they will convince the religious portion of the community that the Reformation was a blunder and a sin. The day cannot be very far off when a direct attack will be made on the Establishment by secularists and infidels, and though the stronghold will not yield to the first attack, it is in the order of things that it must one day go. When it goes, the vast mass of instructed Anglicans will gravitate to Rome. Converts will meanwhile probably become more numerous than they have lately been, as they learn the importance and necessity of a priesthood and the sacraments, and see within their reach certainty and happiness in their quiet possession. Englishmen are slow to learn a truth, and slower still to perceive its bearings and its consequences, but they are honest by nature, and persevering, and true. The Protestant tradition has been broken down, and a vast number of English people are learning the Catholic religion in its place. The Church of England preserved a certain amount of the externals of the Church she supplanted, and now she has appropriated many more. For a time this adopted Catholicism does not seem to some of her own people to be altogether an exotic. But though Ritualism revived an exterior Catholicism in fragmentary and varying measure, consistency and the love of truth will lead men to see what it is and whither it leads. As far as it goes it is God's truth; and parts of God's truth are at home only in God's Church, where His whole truth is to be found. The Church of England cannot remain what it is. It cannot do so, because infidelity is face to face with revelation within her, and the two forces must eventually rend her asunder. It cannot do so, because in accepting revealed doctrine, not as Protestantism was blindly accepted a generation since, but intelligently and with love for it as the ancient truth, that portion or aspect of the Church of England is and must be in a state of transition. The truth, the whole truth, and nothing but the truth is to be found in the Catholic Church only, and each part of the truth has an affinity for the rest. Ritualists will feel that they have either gone too far or not far enough. Those that recede will fall into infidelity, and those that advance will become Catholics. Ritualism is to Catholics very provoking and very ridiculous, but let us never forget that it is training English people to be Catholics. Individuals will come as by God's grace they ripen, and each fresh conversion will make it easier for others. The Church of England puts forth false unauthorized claims, but it is the only religious body in the world that prepares converts for the true faith. We cannot do evil that good may come, and therefore we can do nothing to support the Establishment; but on the other hand we could none of us hasten the day of its downfall. The day however must come in the course of God's providence when the Church of England, that astonishing compromise of English growth, must disappear; and then on one side will be openly arrayed all the forces of unbelief, and on the other every one who believes in the revelation of Christ, gathered within the one fold of the one Shepherd.

And for ourselves, may we not take much comfort from the

way in which God has fought our battle for us, and brought us a harvest to reap that we did not sow? The blood of the Martyrs shed on English soil has kept it fertile, the patience of long generations of confessors of the faith has made God propitious to us. We must and will co-operate with the Divine purposes in behalf of a country we dearly love. God forbid that by our lukewarmness we should be a hindrance in the way of God's good work, or that we should show ourselves unworthy of those who have preserved the Faith alive in the land.

There are dangers for us, beyond a doubt, and of these the greatest is the danger of worldliness. Catholics who for generations had been shut out from what is called Society, are now admitted to it and made flatteringly welcome. The temptation is lest they should rival and outdo the world in its own ways. Those Catholics who would further God's work will gladly avail themselves of their free intercourse to do good, keeping themselves the while, in St. James's words, "unspotted from the world."

Marriage with those who are not Catholics seems to be the rock in the way of our upper as well as of our lower class. Happily some evils connected with it are removed. There was the frightful evil of the partition of the children, to follow the religion of their parents according to their sex. A notable case in Ireland, that led Pius IX. to say that it was against the natural law for a Catholic parent to make such a bargain, was the last instance of anything of the sort being proposed. Another abuse which has disappeared was the performance of the ceremony in the Protestant church, when this was in no way necessary for civil validity and was therefore for religious purposes only. These are gone, but there must always remain a sad division, a lowering of fervour, a danger even of the loss of faith, a lesson of indifference to the children, however conscientious and honourable the Protestant party may be. But surely Catholic girls will be deterred from marrying Protestants by the knowledge that by the law of the land a father cannot contract himself out of his right to prescribe the religion of all his children. And can a Catholic man forget the power that affection gives every mother over her child? In the matter of religion a child is more likely to follow its mother than its father.

For the rest, our prospect, thank God, is bright. Every trace of Jansenism and Gallicanism has disappeared. By far the greatest number of the English Catholics of rank and fortune sided with the Cisalpine Club and the "Protesting Catholic Dissenters" of a century ago, but in our time we might count on the fingers of one hand those that sympathized with Dr. Döllinger and the "Old Catholics." Clergy and laity are thoroughly united in a feeling of perfect loyalty to the Holy See. Internal dissensions have disappeared, and the ancient jealousy between Seculars and Regulars is forgotten. We have a future before us, and we know it. The religious mind of the country is coming round to us, to the surprise of Liberals on the Continent, who recognize the English as a practical people. We must be true to ourselves, and true to God and His Church, and by our love for one another let all men know that we are the disciples of our Lord.

Works on the English Martyrs

BY THE

REV. JOHN MORRIS, S.J.

The Life of Father John Gerard, S.J. Third edition, re-written and enlarged. Demy 8vo. 14s.

Father Morris is one of the few living writers who have succeeded in greatly modifying certain views of English history, which had long been accepted as the only tenable ones. . . . To have wrung an admission of this kind from a reluctant public, never too much inclined to surrender its traditional assumptions, was an achievement not to be underrated in importance. And yet it may be doubted whether Mr. Morris would ever have obtained a hearing at all, or got people to read many pages of the later volumes, if it had not been for the happy chance, or the foreseeing sagacity which induced him to print, as an introduction to the series which was to follow, the remarkable biography which is now re-published as a separate work.—Rev. Augustus Jessopp, D.D., in the *Academy*.

Father Gerard's narrative not only carries on its face all the appearance of artlessness, but its details are so minutely confirmed from contemporary documents, now in the Public Record Office, that a defence of his veracity is wholly unnecessary. . . . The Life is full of interesting particulars, both as regards the writer and many other Jesuits who were employed on the English Mission during the reign of Elizabeth.—*Saturday Review*.

This volume is certainly a literary curiosity. The life of Father Gerard is in the main an autobiography, as full of exciting details as the most sensational of novels. . . . The narrative of the Plot is thoroughly well worth reading, as throwing light on a portion of English history which most students feel has not as yet been thoroughly explored.—*Guardian*.

The autobiography, extending from about 1580 to 1606, should rather be called, "Condition of the Catholics during the latter part of the reign of Queen Elizabeth," of which it presents a very curious and interesting picture. . . . Extreme pains have evidently been taken to render this book as complete as possible.—*Pall Mall Gazette*.

The life is full of the most interesting details of personal adventure and suffering, recounted in the simplest, and therefore in the most telling manner. If any one wants to know what was the life of a Seminary priest in England in the days of Elizabeth, or to visit in imagination the torture-chamber of the Tower or the secret labyrinth of Henlip, he cannot find a better guide than in Mr. Morris's volume.—*Athenæum*.

We have been able to give within our necessary limits but a very imperfect and faint idea of the interest and value of the volume before us, though we have, perhaps, said enough to send our readers to the work itself for a more particular knowledge of its contents; but we cannot conclude without thanking Mr. Morris for his intelligent and unobtrusive editorship, or without speaking highly of the moderate and candid tone of his remarks.—*Spectator*.

Life and Martyrdom of St. Thomas Becket.
Second and enlarged edition. In one vol., large post 8vo, cloth, pp. xxxvi., 632 - - - - - 12s. 6d.
Or bound in two parts. Cloth - - - 13s. 0d.

Father Morris has succeeded in producing a biography worthy of his great and sainted subject. It is full without being voluminous, and possesses all the attractions of an agreeable style. No one can read over its six hundred pages without appreciating the more the saintly grandeur of that character that is there so faithfully described, and at the same time feeling how unjust is the estimate which those have formed of St. Thomas who, as Mr. Froude, have been accustomed to view him as the "proud and ambitious priest." . . . In the Appendix is added a series of historical notes, in which many incidents but briefly referred to in the previous portion of the book are discussed at greater length; as, for instance, the legend of his Saracen parentage, the fate of his murderers, and other subjects of a not less attractive character.—*Irish Ecclesiastical Record.*

The author is especially at home on the congenial subjects of the monasteries and churches which the Saint is said to have visited, of the traces of his presence on the Continent, and of his relics, some of which are extant, though many more have disappeared in "the various storms which have assailed religion." On these topics he brings together information which the ordinary English reader would probably have difficulty in finding elsewhere. . . . Its fulness and precision of details make it a valuable work.—*Saturday Review.*

The services rendered by Father Morris to the Church in connection with the Beatification of the English Martyrs are so remarkable that they are well known not only to Catholics, but to every student of history, as it is now being re-written in the light of the fuller information which was denied to Englishmen of the last generation. . . . For twenty years this admirable book has been out of print, and therefore known only by name to most men of the present generation; and the second and enlarged edition, which is before us, has all the charm of a new work. Father Morris has not written a panegyric, but a faithful biography; he has no theory to support, and his manifest aim has been to tell the plain truth. Hence, as portrayed by him, the career of St. Thomas does not present any of those perplexing problems which beset those who approach the subject under the influence of foregone conclusions. . . . Father Morris has done much more than any previous writer to help to the gradual formation of a correct public opinion on an important period in English Church history. For his co-religionists he has done a service of inestimable value, by giving them a sketch of the life of one of England's greatest Catholic sons that is no less attractive in style than it is accurate in detail. . . . It need only be added that the Notes which compose the Appendix will repay careful study, and that the addition of an excellent Index renders the book most useful for purposes of reference. —*Tablet.*

Two Missionaries under Elizabeth: Father Weston's Narrative, and the Fall of Anthony Tyrrell. Demy 8vo, cloth, 14s.

The Catholics of York under Elizabeth, or Persecution in the North of England. Demy 8vo, cloth, 14s.

These two volumes, each of which is complete in itself, were originally published as the second and third series of *The Troubles of our Catholic Forefathers*, related by themselves; from hitherto unpublished manuscripts.

On the actual working of the penal laws much new information has been given us in the series of contemporary narratives published by Father Morris under the title of *The Troubles of our Catholic Forefathers*.—Mr. John Richard Green, in his *History of the English People*, authorities for Book VI.

Volume after volume of that painful series of *Troubles of our Catholic Forefathers*, which contains some of the most pathetic and some of the most shameful chapters to be found in our country's annals.—Rev. Augustus Jessopp, D.D., in the *Academy*.

The mass of documents which Mr. Morris has printed constitutes a body of evidence which no historian of the sixteenth century can hereafter ignore. If they do not prove that the Catholics were right, they, at any rate, go far to prove that the treatment they endured at the hands of the stronger party was immensely more cruel than was heretofore believed. They reveal a system of the most elaborate espionage that could well be conceived—a truculent barbarity which had hardly been suspected, and an organized persecution, which, as it lasted much longer, so during its course was more crushing and inquisitorial than the previous persecution of Protestants in Queen Mary's days.—*Athenæum*.

Father Morris's second series of *The Troubles of our Catholic Forefathers, related by themselves*, contains two very interesting biographies. The first is the Life of Father William Weston, *alias* Edmunds, taken chiefly from a later autobiography, and carefully completed from two other MS. sources, namely, Grene's collections of Father Parsons's unpublished works at Stonyhurst, and a Spanish Life of Weston by Father de Peralta, a MS. from the Gesù at Rome. Wherever they serve the purpose, the State Papers in the Public Record Office have also been quoted. . . . The second part of Father Morris's book is an autobiographical narrative of the fall of Tyrrell, a Catholic priest who became a hired spy of Elizabeth's Government, and who several times repented and relapsed. . . . What Father Morris—and I must add Brother Foley—have already given us from the treasures of Stonyhurst makes us all the more desirous of further instalments.—Mr. Richard Simpson, in the *Academy*.

Acts of English Martyrs, hitherto unpublished. By Rev. JOHN HUNGERFORD POLLEN, S.J.; with Preface by the Rev. JOHN MORRIS, S.J. Crown 8vo, cloth, 7s. 6d.

The Letter-Books of Sir Amias Poulet,

Keeper of Mary Queen of Scots. 1874. Demy 8vo, cloth; published at 10s. 6d., reduced to 3s. 6d.

We close reluctantly the pages of an interesting and instructive book, of which we can only say that were there more such upon this and kindred historical topics, our history would not labour, as it too frequently does now, under the disadvantage of incomplete or incorrect materials.—*Athenæum.*

In the volume before us are published for the first time a number of letters of Sir Amias which were preserved by his descendants, and are now deposited in the Bodleian Library. Many of these are highly interesting, and Mr. Morris has done good service to the cause of historical truth in placing them before the public. . . . Mr. Morris has both ably and honestly performed his duty as editor of these interesting letters. He is thoroughly acquainted with the history of the period; and in addition to the correspondence of Poulet, he has printed a number of original papers from the Record Office.—Mr. Hosack, in the *Academy.*

These interesting letters, many of which have been hitherto unknown, throw much light on that part of the captivity of Mary Stuart which was passed under the rigorous keeping of Sir Amias Poulet. . . . Mr. Morris deserves the thanks of those students of history who prefer plain facts to picturesque fiction for publishing these very important letters. In editing them he has done his work with great exactness and impartiality.—*Saturday Review.*

In this most interesting volume there is more to be learned of the house life of Mary, during her last years in England, than in any detailed history of her career.—*Notes and Queries.*

The valuable volume of Father Morris on the Letter-Book of Sir Amias Poulet, keeper of Mary Queen of Scots, for extent and originality of research, acuteness of criticism, and breadth and comprehensiveness of view, may claim the very highest rank in the long array of literature, Latin, French, Italian, and English, devoted to the vindication of this ill-fated lady. —The Very Rev. Dr. Russell, President of Maynooth, in the *Dublin Review.*

The Devotions of Lady Lucy Herbert of

Powis, formerly Prioress of the Augustinian Nuns at Bruges. Cloth, gilt, 3s. 6d.

The volume before us contains a great variety of prayers, all of them breathing a spirit of intense piety; and the reflections and meditations with which the book abounds, will render it a favourite in every religious house.—*Weekly Register.*

A very full manual of forms of prayer and meditations, and gives admirable instructions on the latter Divine art. For a long time we have seen nothing which has given us so much pleasure and is calculated to be of greater spiritual profit. Prefixed is a most interesting account of Lady Lucy's Life.—*Church Review.*

London: BURNS AND OATES, Limited.
Roehampton: JAMES STANLEY, Manresa Press.

www.ingramcontent.com/pod-product-compliance
Lightning Source LLC
Chambersburg PA
CBHW022145160426
43197CB00009B/1439